POLICY
PATRONS

THE EDUCATIONAL INNOVATIONS SERIES

The Educational Innovations series explores a wide range of current school reform efforts. Individual volumes examine entrepreneurial efforts and unorthodox approaches, highlighting reforms that have met with success and strategies that have attracted widespread attention. The series aims to disrupt the status quo and inject new ideas into contemporary education debates.

Series edited by Frederick M. Hess

Other books in this series:

The Strategic Management of Charter Schools
by Peter Frumkin, Bruno V. Manno, and Nell Edgington

Customized Schooling
Edited by Frederick M. Hess and Bruno V. Manno

Bringing School Reform to Scale
by Heather Zavadsky

What Next?
Edited by Mary Cullinane and Frederick M. Hess

Between Public and Private
Edited by Katrina E. Bulkley, Jeffrey R. Henig, and Henry M. Levin

Stretching the School Dollar
Edited by Frederick M. Hess and Eric Osberg

School Turnarounds: The Essential Role of Districts
by Heather Zavadsky

Stretching the Higher Education Dollar
Edited by Andrew P. Kelly and Kevin Carey

Cage-Busting Leadership
by Frederick M. Hess

Teacher Quality 2.0: Toward a New Era in Education Reform
Edited by Frederick M. Hess and Michael Q. McShane

Reinventing Financial Aid: Charting a New Course to College Affordability
Edited by Andrew P. Kelly and Sara Goldrick-Rab

The Cage-Busting Teacher
by Frederick M. Hess

Failing Our Brightest Kids: The Global Challenge of Educating High-Ability Students
by Chester E. Finn, Jr. and Brandon L. Wright

The New Education Philanthropy: Politics, Policy, and Reform
Edited by Frederick M. Hess and Jeffrey R. Henig

Educational Entrepreneurship Today
Edited by Frederick M. Hess and Michael Q. McShane

POLICY PATRONS

PHILANTHROPY, EDUCATION REFORM, AND THE POLITICS OF INFLUENCE

Megan E. Tompkins-Stange

HARVARD EDUCATION PRESS
CAMBRIDGE, MASSACHUSETTS

Library of Congress Control Number 2015954225

Paperback ISBN 978-1-61250-912-9
Library Edition ISBN 978-1-61250-913-6

Published by Harvard Education Press,
an imprint of the Harvard Education Publishing Group

Harvard Education Press
8 Story Street
Cambridge, MA 02138

Cover Design: Wilcox Design
Cover Image: iStock.com/Dalton00
The typefaces used in this book are Minion Pro, MetaPlus, and Bodoni

CONTENTS

Foreword   vii
Robert B. Schwartz

1   "Prying Open the Policy Window"   1
    Philanthropic Influence in Education Policy

2   "These Are the New Players"   17
    Continuity and Change in Education Philanthropy

3   "There Are Basically Two Kinds of Foundations"   53
    Conceptualizing Foundations' Policy Involvement

4   "How Do You Establish a Bottom-Up Versus
    Top-Down Mix?"   69
    Managing Grantees and Selecting Partners

5   "We Wish There Was an App for That"   95
    Framing Problems and Evaluating Results

6   "It's Singularly Because of Gates and Broad"   113
    Critiques and Implications of Foundation Activism

7   "Should We Critique the Player or the Game Itself?"   127
    Philanthropy and Democracy

A Note About Methodology   151

Appendix: Table of Respondents   157

References and Notes   159

Acknowledgments   189

About the Author   191

Index   193

FOREWORD

When I joined The Pew Charitable Trusts as Education Program Director in 1990, the first thing I was asked to do was to prepare a white paper proposing a new education strategy for the foundation. As part of that exercise I did a landscape scan, both to find a distinctive niche and to identify potential funding partners who shared my interest in systemic reform, teacher policy, and the transition from high school to college and career. The big players that emerged from that scan, all of whom I would work with in one way or another over the next few years, were Carnegie, MacArthur, Rockefeller, Ford, Hewlett, and Wallace.

Seven years later, when I joined the Harvard Graduate School of Education faculty and was asked what I wanted to teach, I proposed a course on philanthropy and its role in supporting education reform. One frame I used in planning the course was to focus on three competing conceptions of school reform, each vying for primacy with the active backing of major funders. At Pew, we, along with MacArthur and Carnegie, had placed most of our weight behind the standards or systemic reform movement. Funders like Walton, Broad, and the New Schools Venture Fund had put their money mostly behind market-based reform strategies, primarily charter schools. A third set of funders, most notably Atlantic Philanthropies and Rockefeller, had placed their bets on school reform networks led by such notables as Ted Sizer (Coalition of Essential Schools) and James Comer (School Development Program).

From the vantage point of 2015, two things strike me. First, virtually all of the big players I identified in 1990 as leaders have left the K–12 education reform field, including Pew. Only Carnegie remains an active player in that world. The education funding world is now dominated not only by Gates, but by Broad, Walton, Dell, Arnold, and several others that have come into being in the last quarter century and have living donors.

My second observation, not unrelated to the first, is that the competition among the education reform camps is essentially over. The market reformers have won the battle, at least in the eyes of the media, but that has been in some measure because their leaders and funders have come to embrace the core principles of the standards movement. The emergence of the Gates Foundation helped tip the scales here, closely followed by the Obama administration.

The education reform story of the last twenty-five years would look quite different, I suspect, if we hadn't had the emergence of a new generation of activist foundations willing to engage in the public policy arena and use all of the tools at their disposal on behalf of an aggressive reform agenda. When I started to put together a syllabus for "School Reform from the Outside In" (my HGSE course on foundations and school reform), the foundation literature was not of much help. While there were some excellent institutional histories of individual foundations active in education—I think here especially of Ellen Lagemann's volumes on the Carnegie Corporation and the Carnegie Foundation for the Advancement of Teaching—most of the foundation literature fell into two groups: admiring profiles of the brand-name foundations and the generous benefactors who endowed them; or ideologically driven critiques from one side or the other. Critics on the right slammed foundations like Pew for having become too activist and abandoning the conservative principles and values of the founding generation, whereas critics on the left bemoaned the failure of foundations to press a more activist social justice agenda.

About a decade ago the foundation literature began to catch up with the extraordinary changes taking place in the education reform funding landscape with the publication of two excellent edited volumes. As its title suggests, the contributors to *With the Best of Intentions*, edited by Rick Hess, by and large adopt a skeptical stance in assessing the bottom-line impact of the education funding community on the performance of American schools, but the thoughtful and diverse set of contributors recruited by Hess produced a provocative volume that made for lively class discussions. The second volume, *Reconnecting Foundations and Education,* edited by Ray Bachetti and Tom Ehrlich, is a more scholarly volume signaling a growing awareness in the academic community of how some of the more prominent newcomers to the funding world were changing the face of education philanthropy.

Megan Tompkins-Stange is among the leaders of a next generation of young scholars who are probing more deeply into the meaning and consequence of the growing tendency of the new foundations to use their dollars to try to influence public policy. The volume at hand—*Policy Patrons: Philanthropy, Education Reform, and the Politics of Influence*—is a signal contribution to the field. Tompkins-Stange sets out to help us understand these changes in outlook and orientation by contrasting the two most visible and activist newcomers, Gates and Broad, with two of the more established players in the field, Kellogg and Ford. She contrasts these foundations along four dimensions: how they frame problems; how they choose "partners" (her term for grantees); how they manage their grantees; and how they evaluate results. In her analysis, one pair frames problems as essentially technical; the other, as adaptive. One pair tends to seek out "grasstop" grantees; the other, more grassroots organizations. One pair manages its grantees in a more controlling fashion; the other, more trusting and laissez-faire. And one pair generally opts for quantitative evaluation of results; the other, mixed methods. As with any typology, one can always think of cases that don't neatly seem to fit the frame, but on balance the frame is a useful one in analyzing the work of different types of foundations.

For me, the most interesting of the contrasts she draws is in how these foundations manage their grantees. While some of the older, more established foundations may be less strategic in their grant making than the newcomers, by and large they pride themselves on supporting ideas and initiatives that come from the field and they don't try to micromanage their grantees. If there is a sin that besets some of the newcomers, it is hubris. They think they are the ones with the answers, so they design their own initiatives and then seek out organizations to carry out these ideas. This approach blurs the line between contracting and grant making. If you choose a contractor and manage his or her performance against the contract, you are likely to get compliance, not creativity, and technical rather than adaptive responses to the unanticipated challenges that inevitably rise in the course of complex projects.

What makes Tompkins-Stange's book so compelling is her methodology. She somehow managed to persuade sixty foundation insiders, including senior people from these four foundations, to sit for extensive interviews, and because she promised them anonymity, they are for the most part remarkably candid. As in virtually all conversations about education funders, the Gates Foundation gets the lion's share of the attention from Tompkins-Stange's informants. Given its size and influence, Gates is endlessly fascinating to foundation watchers, and it is clear from these interviews that folks inside the foundation are asking many of the same questions that those of us outside ask, questions that get to the heart of the relationship between foundations and democracy.

While Tompkins-Stange does her best to maintain an even-handed stance, she seems more attuned philosophically to the less prescriptive, more bottom-up approach to grant making that she ascribes to Kellogg and Ford. I'm an admirer of much of what Gates and Broad have accomplished through their grant making, but with Gates especially, its sheer size can't help raising concerns when it enters the public policy arena. As the question is sometimes put, "Who elected these guys?"

Tompkins-Stange's concluding advice is for foundations at least to be aware of this normative question about the role of foundations in the democratic marketplace as they consider undertaking initiatives aimed at affecting public policy. Whatever your views about the proper role of foundations in attempting to influence public policy in education, you'll find this a stimulating and provocative read.

Robert B. Schwartz
Senior Research Fellow
Harvard Graduate School of Education

Foundation involvement in public controversies [is]
one of the major questions regarding the nature and
role foundations should play in American life. . . .
If foundations should endeavor to have a more direct
impact on contemporary problems, how deeply should
they become involved?

—HEIMANN, 1973

1

"Prying Open the Policy Window"

Philanthropic Influence in Education Policy

To begin this examination of philanthropic influence in US education policy, consider four recent developments. In 2011, the Los Angeles Unified School District adopted a "value-added" approach to teacher evaluation, assessing teacher quality based on students' standardized test scores. In 2010, the Washington, DC, teacher union contract introduced teacher merit pay, wherein "highly effective" teachers received bonuses outside of standard union pay schedules. In 2013, a series of schools in New York City instituted a longer instructional day and year with higher teacher compensation. And in 2009, nearly all US governors entered a compact to pursue a standardized curriculum for K–12 education—the beginning of the Common Core.

What do these seemingly distinct initiatives have in common? Each represents a major policy change, with significant impact on how core educational goals are delivered—how teachers are evaluated and paid; how school time is organized and allocated; and how states deliver educational content and determine student readiness. But more importantly, each policy change was championed and partially funded by private philanthropic foundations.

Philanthropic involvement in policy arenas is not new; indeed, foundations have exercised influence in public policy since their origins in the early twentieth century. But the past two decades represent a watershed change in the visibility and centrality of philanthropy within public education. In 1995, just 16 private foundations held more than $1 billion in assets, while an additional 164 held more than $100 million; by 2010, these numbers had tripled, with 42 foundations holding assets of $1 billion or more, and an additional 556 holding more than $100 million. Moreover, large foundations are more likely than their smaller peers to value policy influence as a strategic priority.[1] As private wealth has risen, so has public critique about the role of influence of foundations in the public arena, and as a result, foundations remain guarded against the threat of possible reputational damage. In this context, which Joel Fleishman terms a "culture of diffidence," relatively little is known about the internal processes, norms, and values that motivate foundations' attempts to influence policy—a significant void.[2]

In this book, I offer a unique look inside the closed world of foundations, exploring how four of the largest and most powerful foundations in the United States—the Gates Foundation, the Broad Foundation, the Kellogg Foundation, and the Ford Foundation—have attempted to generate change in education policy. (Throughout the following pages, the foundations are identified as "Gates," "Broad," "Kellogg," and "Ford.") In Chapter 2, I describe the four foundations' organizational histories, and review how each foundation approaches policy influence. In Chapter 3, I present a conceptual framework that illustrates two contrasting modes of policy engagement, which I term *outcome-oriented* and *field-oriented* approaches. In chapters 4 and 5, I illustrate how these approaches contrast along four dimensions: how grantees are managed, how partners are selected, how problems are framed, and how outcomes are evaluated. In Chapter 6, I consider the implications of these different approaches for the field of education, and in Chapter 7, I reflect on what these findings contribute to discussions about the legitimacy of foundations' policy influence within a liberal democracy.

"Who's the Hub?"

This story, at its outset, is my own. A decade ago, I did some contract work for a private foundation that made grants to K–12 education (a foundation that will remain nameless and vaguely described, for reasons explained in the following pages). For the five years prior, this foundation had funded an initiative to influence education policy at the state level. The foundation carefully assembled a grant portfolio of about one hundred grantees, including organizations that varied from think tanks to grassroots advocacy groups. By funding this diverse group of grantees, the foundation sought to catalyze what one staff member called "a social movement towards a massive policy reform"—a social movement of the foundation's own design. Publicly, foundation staff members described this effort as "building political will." Privately, they called it "prying open a policy window."

The foundation faced a number of challenges in managing this intentional movement. While the grantees were united by their interest in pursuing the targeted educational reforms, for which the foundation had sought them out, they had weak ties to one another, and in many cases lacked shared professional history or personal relationships. This diffusion of grants across a wide variety of fields was intentional on the foundation's part, as staff sought to "foment the movement [through] different groups," in the words of one foundation official. As a result, though, foundation staff struggled with the degree of control they could—or should—exert in order to strategically shape the grantees into a functioning policy network. Should they anoint an exemplary grantee as the de facto leader of the initiative, or should the grantees organically determine their own leaders and direction? One foundation official remarked on the challenges of orchestrating these decisions from the funder's perspective:

> *There's a tension [when we] try to control and direct everything. [For example], [putting] certain contingencies on the funding— "We'll fund this if you do X." Or "Collaborate with this group that you don't even like. If you're willing to collaborate, we'll give you money." It's well intentioned, but it's like dating. You can't force two people to date that don't want to.*

The alternative approach, however, also presented challenges. In theory, the foundation found a bottom-up approach more resonant with its values, as one official explained:

> *It keeps the accountability on everybody to figure out who should be the hub ... [it creates] a continued competitive incentive for everyone to perform. There should be some organic leadership that evolves if this turns into a movement—it's better for us to wait and watch and listen until it's obvious who the organic leader is. We haven't seen anyone who's worth placing a big bet on yet—the "this is it, this is the organic hub."*

However, when the foundation elected to follow this strategy, and let leadership emerge organically rather than being determined from the top down, grantees did indeed become competitive with one another, but not always with the positive benefits the foundation had envisioned. One foundation official commented on this dynamic:

> *All the groups are saying there's not enough coordination, there's no "hub"—they don't have enough information about what everybody else is doing. Groups in the field say they don't know how to plug in—[They're saying,] "Who should I get in touch with to become part of this movement?" And groups that are more plugged in want to be the leader and to not be controlled. Everyone wants to have their* thing be the one.

In numerous conversations, foundation staff pondered, "Who's the hub?" and "Should there be a hub?" while occasionally fielding bids from grantees entreating them to "Make us the hub," as one staff member detailed:

> *[One particularly visible grantee] told us, "Just pick me—I'm in charge." [So do we] pronounce to everyone that [this grantee is] the hub, with [the foundation's] legitimacy [backing them]? There's no externally valid reason why some groups should have to follow the lead of others. We can't identify one group as the leader—people want their thing to win. Every time we pick a hub it always fails. Everyone has something to be mad about because the other ninety-nine groups didn't get picked.*

Over eighteen months, I observed these conversations and many others, watching as the foundation made incremental progress in its goals—through convening grantees, meetings with state government officials, and coordinating messaging and public relations efforts with media and professional consultants. Throughout these observations, I was most intrigued by the way that the foundation negotiated its role as a private organization operating in the public sphere. Staff members were assertive about advancing the foundation's priorities to the greatest extent possible, yet conscious of being too directive or overt in the process. One staff member commented about the "honest broker" role that the foundation sought to maintain:

> *This role that we are carving out on [education policy]—we don't just say, "You have to reform in this way; X model is the perfect model." Instead we have said, "This area is a major problem—[this policy] is a mess." It wasn't on anyone's agenda—we put this on the agenda, but we are maintaining our neutral broker role. It's not our perfect solution but it's a solution—it enables us to keep our honest broker role while still being more aggressive about pushing for a specific area.*

This "aggressive" advocacy paid off for the foundation, as several of its signature initiatives were successfully promoted in policy circles during the duration of its sponsorship. Although its efforts were eventually stymied by the financial crisis in 2008, the foundation was considered successful in advancing some of its goals, as an independent evaluation of this work determined the following:

> [The foundation] has played a critical role in strengthening the field of education and supporting efforts that contributed toward significant policy changes in [the state] . . . there is no other player, private or public, to take on [the foundation]'s role in galvanizing stakeholders and pushing toward systemic changes in education that would ultimately impact all [state residents].

Witnessing this impact, and the access that the foundation had to policy makers by virtue of its financial resources and political connections, led me to a significant realization: behind the management issues the foundation faced were even deeper normative questions about the role of foundations in a liberal democracy. Did the foundation's advancement of its educational aims align with the preferences of the broader public? Was it beneficial for democracy to have a powerful institution like the foundation push an otherwise ignored issue onto the political agenda and martial its considerable resources toward addressing it in a far more agile way than the government? Could these actions be seen as detrimental, elevating the preferences of private interests with few structured accountability mechanisms? And did foundations' power to advance certain solutions to public problems have the potential to influence policy and practice without a single vote being cast?

"I TRUST THE BILLIONAIRES"

At the time, few seemed to care much about these questions. In discussions with a variety of philanthropic officials, practitioners, and policy-related actors from 2006 to 2011, I found that the overarching attitude toward normative questions about foundation involvement in policy contexts was remarkably blasé and often dismissed as an academic exercise. One source stated, "Most people think foundations are on the side of the angels," while another explained, "They're doing work that everybody on the receiving end believes is good, and because everybody likes the largesse, it's just under-scrutinized." One Gates staff member remarked on the widespread admiration for the foundation that she had experienced: "It's almost uncomfortable; there's a reverence and a belief that the foundation just knew so much more than anyone else, and a bowing to the power." The common rationale for foundation involvement in policy was expressed as follows: *Foundations are able to achieve positive policy outcomes in a manner that is far more efficient than the bureaucratic state, and thus their involvement in policy is beneficial.* In this argument, foundations were viewed as legitimate players in policy contexts if they produced impact. Essentially, foundations traded on output legitimacy, or the extent to which they produced impactful, efficient, and effective policy change, as opposed to their input legitimacy, or the extent to which they reflected the representative or authentic views of the public.[3]

This rationale reflected widespread attitudes among the public and press during this time period, which was particularly evident following Warren Buffett's landmark $31 billion gift to the Gates Foundation in 2006. The gift was described in the press using almost exclusively celebratory terms, and, as Bruce Sievers wrote in a lonely contrarian opinion, with limited analysis of the implications of concentrating an unprecedented amount of philanthropic wealth in a single foundation.[4] Rick Cohen wrote that the overall reception to Buffett's gift represented "blind faith in the plutocrats"—a characterization that I vividly remember, as a student I taught in 2007 somewhat dismissively responded to another student's critique of Gates's amplified wealth with the statement, written on a class blog, "I trust the billionaires."[5]

Then, around 2011, something changed—triggered, somewhat ironically, by the amplified size and influence of the Gates Foundation. Critiques of philanthropic involvement in policy began to emerge in the press, slowly but steadily, as Gates and other national foundations—most notably Broad and Walton—began to attract attention for their vocal and visible role in federal education reform. The media began to espouse views that were once considered the realm of conspiracy theory; indeed, as one source (who self-identified on the "radical" end of the spectrum in his views toward philanthropy) reflected in the summer of 2014, "Our views are now mainstream."

These more critical views soon became caricatured, however. The emergent narrative centered on a handful of elite, high-endowment and high-engagement foundations—notably Gates, Broad, and Walton—that had wrested hold of federal education policy and imposed their views upon the polity. While this critical and somewhat sensational narrative was certainly compelling from a popular media perspective, in reality, the story was much more nuanced.

A FIGURATIVE COVER OF DARKNESS

This story developed over the course of nearly nine years, from 2006 to 2015, as I sought to understand, illustrate, and analyze philanthropic involvement in education policy. I conducted sixty in-depth interviews with high-level foundation insiders at Gates, Broad, Kellogg, and Ford, in addition to grantees, academics, and leaders in the fields of philanthropy and education. These interviews yielded unusually rich and unique qualitative data that illustrates the internal dynamics, politics, and perspectives of contemporary foundation officials, offering a new viewpoint into norms, values, and decisions within guarded institutional environments.

These findings are compelling because they are so rare, since access to foundations' inner workings is often restricted. Foundations' actions are frequently opaque, concealed in order to protect against legal and reputational risk. Hoffman and Schwartz describe this dynamic in the following way: "to seal the curtain around foundations, good program officers are schooled in decorum. They are socialized to be pleasant, to listen well and respectfully, and not to disclose doubt, confusion, or dis-satisfaction."[6] Numerous researchers have experienced foundation pro-gram officers being guarded about the information they divulge about their work, which in some cases has limited scholarship about philan-thropy.[7] As a result, empirical research on the policy activities of con-temporary foundations—particularly the concrete mechanisms and processes, or ways in which foundations attempt to accomplish policy influence—has been limited until only the last decade.[8]

Part of this limitation is no doubt caused by self-policing on the part of researchers; for example, in 2011, Timothy Ogden guest-edited a spe-cial issue of *Alliance*, a leading nonprofit sector publication, which criti-cally analyzed the implications of Gates's influence on a variety of fields. Nearly half of the potential contributors he asked to participate chose not to, citing fear for their professional reputations and potential future access to grants. As such, until the last several years, research on foun-dations' policy influence has predominantly been historical, conducted via archival analysis or retrospective interviews several decades after central staff members have departed or key actors have passed away.[9]

To move beyond the party line, and to enable foundation staff to feel comfortable speaking with me, I chose to protect the anonymity of the people I interviewed. When I began to pursue this research as a grad-uate student, some faculty were concerned about my ability to secure access to interview subjects, which they believed represented one of the more impenetrable groups I could pursue—doubly so, given my desire to conduct interviews with high-level officials. Whether through arro-gance or naiveté, I persisted with this line of inquiry, taking precautions to protect foundation employees' confidentiality—and sometimes meeting under a figurative cover of darkness, at neutral locations away from informants' offices. Throughout the book, I have redacted all identifiable details about individual sources, and sometimes use generic descriptors like "informants," "interviewees," or "respon-dents," as well as terms like "the official" or "the staff member." Thus, the ensuing narrative occasionally assumes a rather dramatic tone (in fact, one former Gates Foundation official who reviewed one chapter at a conference stated that while she read, she pictured my "informants" with the visage of the tragic confidential informant, Bubbles, from *The Wire*, a reference that will not be lost on devoted fans of the storied HBO show).

Guaranteeing anonymity in this way has obvious drawbacks. I was not able to be granular in my description of the interviewees' backgrounds, which required the exclusion of a significant amount of relevant information, but I determined it was necessary to increase access to sources and to protect interviewees from any possible professional, legal, or reputational risk. Ensuring the respondents' anonymity appears to have enabled the interview subjects to be refreshingly candid regarding their work, thoughtfully reflecting on the foundations' strategies as well as sharing their own thoughts about the role of foundations in public policy. In fact, in response to a question about philanthropic engagement in a democratic society, one source shared, "That's a question I haven't indulged in," before beginning a two-hour conversation about the topic. My sense is that, in fact, most of the interviewees have not typically "indulged" in these questions and were excited when given the opportunity to do so. Thus, this work offers a unique viewpoint from foundation officials in contemporary foundations, reflecting on their work, often in real time, in highly nuanced, dynamic, and multifaceted philanthropic contexts.

PHILANTHROPY IN THE PUBLIC REALM

Historically, Americans have been wary of foundations' use of private wealth to advance ideas that impact the broader public, without the accountability provided by formal democratic processes. In fact, foundations have been at the center of periodic contentious political debate about the impact of private wealth within the public realm for over a century.[10] Private foundations possess a unique combination of financial resources and political privileges that confer social prestige and legitimacy on their actions, lending them influence in the public arena.[11] In the United States, the prominence of foundations was borne of America's historical reliance on private charity rather than the state to provide public welfare, often through religious organizations focused on almsgiving and the amelioration of suffering, in a distinct contrast to other modern democracies' state-centric provision of social needs.[12] In the early 1900s, in the context of massive immigration, urban poverty, and industrialization, charitable providers' capacity was exhausted, and new professional grant-making institutions emerged. These institutions differed significantly from the charitable enterprises of the early republic—not only in scale and scope, but also their emphasis on influencing public policy, which was viewed as a necessary lever to target the root causes of complex social challenges rather than addressing their effects.[13]

Foundations' engagement in policy contexts originated during the era of "scientific philanthropy" in the Progressive period in the early 1900s, when social reformers sought to professionalize, systematize, and rationalize social welfare provision.[14] By investing in research and supporting elite universities and think tanks,[15] foundations aimed to develop rigorous empirical expertise to inform policy makers' decisions.[16,17] Foundations also incubated novel social initiatives called "demonstration projects," or pilot sites intended to eventually be scaled more broadly via state adoption.[18] Perhaps the most well-known historical example of a demonstration project is the Rockefeller Foundation's pursuit of the eradication of hookworm, through the privately funded Rockefeller Sanitary Commission in 1909, which was one of the United States' first major broad-scale public health interventions, and was later institutionalized in government as the US Sanitary Commission. In the words of Frederick Gates, principal philanthropic advisor to John D. Rockefeller from 1891 to 1923, the hookworm intervention was commissioned "under the guise of the state health boards, while it is in fact minutely directed and paid for by the Rockefeller Commission."[19]

Fifty years later, the Ford Foundation developed new models of social service delivery through the Gray Areas program, which aimed to target urban social blight by creating economic development opportunities in impoverished neighborhoods.[20] In 1955, the program's director, Paul Ylvisaker, determined that Ford's Gray Areas program would "create the new institutional forms that would make government work."[21] The Gray Areas model was incorporated into the Economic Opportunity Act of 1964, positioning the Ford Foundation as a central actor in liberal policy throughout the 1960s.[22,23]

Ford's actions in the late 1950s and 1960s provide an example of a foundation engaging in what Teles terms "strategic coordination," acting as a central node in a policy network, using its own political capital to leverage change as opposed to operating primarily through grantees.[24] This visible activism contrasted with the more hands-off investments that characterized more traditional philanthropic policy influence strategies, or what former Ford Foundation director Paul Yvislaker described as "philanthropic detachment."[25] Ford's high-profile actions had consequences for foundations as political actors more generally, however: by the late 1960s, significant controversy about Ford's, and by extension, other foundations' policy-related activities emerged in Congress, a recurrent pattern throughout the history of modern philanthropy.

Since their earliest origins, foundations have been consistently criticized for their involvement in policy matters and viewed with suspicion as potential sites of dissident power wielded by unelected elites.[26] Congress investigated foundations' policy-related activities in three separate waves of inquiry, beginning in 1908, when John D. Rockefeller sought a public charter of incorporation for his new charitable foundation at the same time that his company, Standard Oil, was under fire for abusive labor practices. In 1912, the Commission on Industrial Relations formed the Walsh Commission to officially address these issues, concluding in 1916: "A small group of wealthy families not only control the major industries but also worked at extending that control over education and social services . . . through the creation of enormous privately managed funds for indefinite purposes, hereinafter designated 'foundations.'" In 1915, the Commission's namesake, Congressman Frank Walsh, argued against foundation involvement in public concerns:

Even if the great charitable and philanthropic trusts should con-
fine their work to the field of science, where temperament, point of
view, and economic theory cannot enter, many of us should still
feel that this was work for the state, and that even in the power to
do good, no one man, or group of men should hold the monopoly.[27]

Thirty years later, during early 1950s McCarthyism, foundations were accused of fomenting Communism and sabotaging the US economy as "seed-beds of subversion," in stark contrast to earlier concerns about robber barons' capitalistic abuses.[28] A decade later, in 1961, foundations were again on the political agenda, as Congress made extensive inquiries into foundations' fiduciary malfeasance, tax harboring, and political overreaching. This research resulted in Congressional hearings on the Tax Reform Act in 1969, which focused on foundations' illegal behavior, converging on the progressive political activities of the Ford Foundation around civil rights and racial equity. The hearings resemble a soap opera, rife with heightened emotion on the part of Congress, whose members were most incensed about the potential for foundations to fund their challengers in elections. The *Congressional Record* summarized the episode as follows: "[Congress] members termed some foundations 'holding companies' for out-of-power government officials, and charged that the influence of powerful foundations constituted a sub-government that swayed the thinking of legislators and executive branch officials."[29,30,31]

As a result of the hearings, watershed legal regulations were enacted, prohibiting foundations from acting as "direct agents of influence" on legislation, "influencing the outcome of any specific political campaign," communicating with legislators regarding specific policy measures, or endorsing legislation. While foundations could fund 501(c)3 public charities, which were permitted to engage in a limited amount of lobbying, they could not direct their grantees to lobby, and foundations themselves could not lobby at all.[32] Although these restrictions appeared rigid, the term "direct agents of influence" was sufficiently ambiguous to allow a wide scope of latitude, and foundations continued to pursue—and in some cases accelerate—policy-related activities after the act's passage in 1969, often labeling their efforts in neutral terms such as "educating the public," "convening stakeholders," "raising awareness," and "supporting implementation."[33,34,35,36]

The Tax Reform Act led foundations to become more cautious regarding disclosure of their internal activities, and averse to supporting more politically overt or grassroots social movement organizations, preferring instead to invest in noncontroversial groups.[37, 38, 39] In 1973, Simon summarized the effect of the Tax Reform Act in the immediate aftermath of its passage:

> In the Act, a kind of floating mine is present in the form of the provision, which inhibits foundations from using their tax-free funds to "influence any legislation through an attempt to affect the opinion of the general public or any segment thereof." So far this and other provisions of the Act bearing upon the political behavior of foundations have been broadly interpreted and have not—it is generally agreed—much inhibited the activities of the foundations. That floating mine in the Act is therefore, as it were, unarmed; but it is also clear that any unduly risqué political initiative on the part of the foundations would result in the prompt arming of that floating mine.[40]

To date, no foundation has ever been censured for its policy-related activity; thus, the extent to which this legislation has actually impacted philanthropic practice is not well understood. Rumors periodically circulate in the philanthropic community about the risk of governmental scrutiny, however, and whether through self-regulation or the possibility of external censure, the impact of the Tax Reform Act of 1969 remains, to varying degrees, alive and well in the foundation field.

WHAT DOES "POLICY" MEAN?

Given the ambiguous legal environment that foundations have existed in for over four decades, the meaning of "policy" has been interpreted broadly. What exactly do foundations mean when they talk about "policy influence," "policy engagement," or "policy and advocacy work"? At the outset of my research, I thought about "policy influence" in a highly traditional way—as any effort to shape or change legislation, as expressed in actual laws, whether at the local, state, or policy level. I soon learned, however, that many foundations were not concerned with legislation at all. In fact, foundations tend to conceptualize "policy" in a much broader way than traditional ways of assessing policy influence allow, viewing "policy activities" as including such strategies as developing new professional communities of practice, changing debates and conversations about policy issues at a national level, or illustrating best practices in the administration of public organizations, rather than primarily intending to affect legislative output. Foundations' activities are as diverse as funding a research project or publishing a book, convening a commission or a group of advocates, spearheading a public information program, or offering technical assistance to government committees.

These change mechanisms, or what Lagemann describes as "technologies of influence," vary substantially among foundations.[41] Whereas some take a more indirect approach, investing in research, expertise building, and support for knowledge capital, others act more directly, engaging in closely coupled relationships with policy makers and building coalitions of elites to advocate for specific goals. Traditionally, foundations that have pursued more indirect routes of influencing policy have been termed "honest" or "neutral" brokers—predominantly serving a convening or linking function, but stopping short of direct involvement in policy.[42] In contrast, other foundations take a more direct, agentic approach, pursuing policy influence using their own brands and institutional legitimacy rather than primarily operating through giving grants to other organizations. As I will show in the following chapters, foundations' approaches toward policy activities are a function of their most fundamental institutional histories, cultures, and values, and in turn, have significant implications for education policy and practice.

Deepening the Debate

By better understanding how contemporary foundations aim to influence policy, and weighing the costs and benefits of their different approaches, I aim to inform current debates about the role of foundations in public policy. Importantly, I attempt to do so in a tempered way, as these debates are rarely conducted in "measured tones," as Carr states.[43] Foundations are alternatively lauded and censured, celebrated and critiqued for their policy influence, and these discussions are often based on ideology rather than empirical rigor. As public interest in the political activity of foundations has renewed in the past several years, and particularly as the relationship between philanthropy and inequality has come into sharp relief in national politics, these discussions deserve to be deepened. And there is no better context for this discussion than the field of public education, which has undergone what Janelle Scott calls a "paradigmatic shift" sparked in large part by the influence of the new foundations.[44] In the next chapter, I introduce the four foundations and discuss how their organizational histories, strategic priorities, and valued expertise have shaped their views towards influencing policy.

2

"These Are the New Players"

Continuity and Change in Education Philanthropy

A rguably, no social sector in the United States is more heavily impacted by foundations than K–12 education. Foundation funding to education has nearly quadrupled during the last three decades, representing a significant infusion of capital. Foundation dollars have amplified influence in education, since these funding streams are not constrained in the same manner as public dollars, and can be targeted in a discretionary fashion toward initiatives that the state cannot support. For example, the superintendent of Newark's public school system, Cami Anderson, noted in a 2011 *New York Times* article: "We're not thinking about philanthropic dollars as a replacement for public dollars. We are thinking about using it for things that need to be accelerated—where only private dollars can uniquely facilitate innovation because of the restrictions in government money sources."[1]

Philanthropic interest in social improvement through education has a long history since the post–Civil War era. During the Reconstruction era, the first two organized philanthropic trusts in the nation's history, the Peabody Fund and the Rosenwald Fund, were founded to provide support for universal public education for black children, in partnership with southern governments.[2,3] Large philanthropic investments in education continued throughout the next century, most notably the Annenberg Challenge, a $500 million gift made by Walter Annenberg in 1993, which represented the largest philanthropic grant to education in history.[4] In the more than twenty years since the Annenberg Challenge, philanthropists and critics have widely cited it as a failure, due to its dilution of capital across too many school districts, resulting in a lack of concentrated impact. Consequently, they have planned initiatives that are explicitly designed to avoid the Challenge's pitfalls.

Prior to the 1990s, the most active education funders were located predominantly on the East Coast and were founded in the early half of the twentieth century (for example, Annenberg, Carnegie, and Ford); however, during the last fifteen years, a number of younger foundations have risen to prominence, including several located on the West Coast, in what Hess calls a "changing of the guard."[5] These "new" philanthropists differ qualitatively from the older foundations, as new education funders are interested in accomplishing concrete outcomes that yield significant return on investment, often organized around initiatives that reflect market-based values, such as choice and competition.[6] One respondent, a senior official at a philanthropic consulting firm, described these differences: "Fifteen or twenty years ago, [the big player] was Annenberg; now it's Gates and Broad. They have different priorities."

THE FOUR FOUNDATIONS

To examine these institutional differences, I studied four of the twenty largest philanthropies that are active in the education sector: the Gates Foundation, Broad Foundation, Kellogg Foundation, and Ford

Foundation (see Table 2.1). Whereas Gates and Broad are both "new foundations," founded in the last fifteen years, Kellogg and Ford represent an older cohort, with founding dates in the 1930s. Although all four foundations consider policy influence as central to their organizational cultures, they vary in the degree to which they are comfortable with making those values visible to the public, ranging from being overt and aggressive to "under the radar" in terms of their actions in the policy realm. Whereas Gates is now an active policy funder, it was initially reticent about political involvement of any kind, and over the fifteen years of its existence, it has embraced policy as a central lever yet remains highly cautious about legal regulations. In contrast, Kellogg has been highly committed to policy influence throughout its nearly ninety-year history yet has also been cautious about the ramifications of its activities, similar to Gates. Until the past five years, it has predominantly operated behind the scenes, reluctant to engage its own brand publicly as a visible advocate and preferring to advance its goals through its grantees' activities. Conversely, Broad and Ford have both viewed policy influence as a central priority since their earliest days of existence, and maintain organizational identities as active and visible policy actors, yet express these identities in significantly different ways.

TABLE 2.1   The four foundations

	Bill and Melinda Gates Foundation	Eli and Edythe Broad Foundation	W. K. Kellogg Foundation	Ford Foundation
Date of founding	2000	1999	1930	1936
Size of endowment (2015)	$41.3 billion	$2.6 billion	$7.3 billion	$12.4 billion
Geographic location	Seattle, WA	Los Angeles, CA	Battle Creek, MI	New York, NY

Bill and Melinda Gates Foundation

The Gates Foundation was founded in 2000 in Seattle, Washington, with a mission to "help reduce inequities in the United States and around the world." The foundation's benefactors, Bill and Melinda Gates, accumulated their wealth through the Microsoft Corporation, which Bill Gates founded and served as CEO for nearly thirty years. In 2006, Warren Buffett, chairman of Berkshire Hathaway, joined Gates as a third benefactor, contributing $31 billion as a personal gift to the foundation. Gates's endowment of $41.3 billion renders it the largest actor in the field of US education philanthropy; by comparison, its next largest peer, the Ford Foundation, has a $12.4 billion endowment.

Gates's education program, and its organizational structure as a whole, has undergone significant change since its founding. The foundation's grant-making programs were originally organized around four distinct topical categories (global health, education, libraries, and the Pacific Northwest), which were reorganized in 2005 into national initiatives primarily focusing on education and international initiatives centering on global health. Prior to 2006, when Warren Buffett made the $31 billion gift to Gates, the foundation disbursed $1.5 billion in grants annually. Buffett stipulated that, following two years of preparation and staffing increases, Gates would be required to pay out an additional $1.5 billion per year, or an average of $8 million a day, by 2008.

From its beginning, Gates's strategy involved the investment of large amounts of capital in projects with aggressive timelines, which was a necessity in order to meet its mandated annual payout requirement of 5 percent of its endowment. The transition period after the Buffett gift had a significant effect on Gates's organizational culture and structure. Gates was initially committed to maintaining a lean organizational structure, maintaining a relatively small staff and relying on external partnerships with intermediaries to manage grantees. After the Buffett gift, the Gates organization struggled as the workload doubled in size, as one staff member described:

How do you take an organization that was doing three or four things in a deep and engaged way, many well, but not all of them, and then try all of a sudden to double the number of people, double the grant making?

The challenges associated with this rapid growth persisted, as one source noted in 2012: "They're choking. [A senior Gates staffer] told me, 'That money is the worst thing that ever happened to us.' They went from two hundred employees to seven hundred employees in a year." A former staff member noted, "People's jobs [at Gates] were being redefined about every three months. They were just in constant turmoil. Organizationally, they were trying to figure out what their theory of action was." Another Gates official explained: "The foundation is an organization where the perspectives, philosophies, strategies, and culture shifts pretty rapidly."

This culture of rapid change was manifested in the education program's approach toward grant making. Gates's first major education effort in the early 2000s was widely known as the "small schools" initiative, wherein the foundation granted $1.3 billion to redesign large comprehensive high schools and create smaller learning communities. In 2005 and 2006, indicators emerged that the initiative was not meeting benchmarks of progress, including a high-profile failure of Manual High School in Denver, Colorado, where Gates had donated $1 million.[7] These results led a number of critics to question the foundation's small schools initiative. One Gates staff member explained this process:

Breaking existing schools into smaller schools is incredibly difficult on many levels. In [one state], I think at least all eight of the big urban districts that participated in the initiative had five of their eight high schools breaking up. Every single one of those high schools had reverted back to a comprehensive.

After a 2006 evaluation indicated that the small schools portfolio was not achieving the results the foundation desired, Gates decided to change course, shifting its resources to a new strategy that emphasized systemic reform at the district, state, and national levels. One former Gates official recalled, "One of the things they learned, which is a very powerful lesson, [was] that the structural reform was not enough, and they needed to go much deeper into a more thorough reform." Similarly, a Gates staff member said: "[We decided] we can't just be about giving dollars to school districts because we've already seen evidence that we give money and we're not seeing results." Another staffer corroborated, "I think one of the key lessons learned is that you can spend three to five years just focusing on the structure and not getting to the substance of improving instruction and student engagement. We could see the handwriting on the wall." During this time, according to one official, Gates realized that educational change "involved much more than structure; it needed to involve the context, the policy context, that affected it."

In 2006, Gates began to pursue comprehensive systemic standards-based school reform efforts that aligned with federal and state policy measures under the 2001 federal No Child Left Behind Act, with a focus on teacher quality–related reforms and standardized state curricular standards and assessments. With this strategic shift in 2006, policy initiatives assumed a new importance, as one former Gates staffer described: "Gates had a very explicit theory of action about working at the state level to create a policy environment that would be supportive of the kinds of changes that they wanted to make." Another former staffer explained the foundation's changing strategy: "The reason they've gone to [this] approach is because they really understood that the work they were doing needed to address some of the ways in which human capital was recruited, managed, and deployed." This new understanding was driven by significant research into teacher effectiveness, some of which Gates funded directly through the Measures of Effective Teaching project, a landmark study conducted under the direction of Harvard professor Tom Kane. One staff member described Gates's new focus on teacher effectiveness as a function of its investments in research:

We went back to the research, and the research is really clear that effective teaching is the single greatest variable for student outcomes. We tried a whole bunch of other stuff and it still comes back to if you have a highly effective teacher, then outcomes of students are a whole lot better; and if you don't, then they're worse; and what we don't know though is what makes a teacher effective. And so we have hundreds of millions of dollars in research now going on, trying to figure that out.

Another Gates official described how these investments in research informed their strategic choices in policy:

Back in the old days, we had a whole policy team and we did our policy platform and we had comments and positions on the important policy issues in education of the day. "So what do you think about choice? What did you think about charters?" Which I think now is the wrong question. Instead, it should be "What does it take to scale and sustain those practices that radically improve student outcomes?" Now we really are bringing our research to bear on this question of how do you increase the effectiveness of teachers and particularly the access of poor children to highly effective teachers.

One respondent, a Gates grantee, lauded the foundation's investment in research in this area:

There are some big, important intellectual efforts right now that the Gates Foundation is working on in teacher quality. They're putting a ton of money in what amounts to basic research trying to understand teacher quality. Frankly, in a better world, it would be the federal government that is putting hundreds of millions of dollars in that. But they don't because it all goes to [entitlements] or it's politicized.

Along with investments in research, Gates funded perhaps its signature initiative under its structural reform strategy—a compact among

US governors to support national instructional standards, called the Common Core, in order to standardize academic requirements across all fifty states. Led by Gates's director of policy and advocacy, Stefanie Sanford, in close partnership with its grantee, the National Governors Association, this effort was seen by many respondents as the beginning of Gates's dominance in education policy debates at a national level. One Gates official described this development:

> Stefanie really led this effort around a compact with the governors, and that's where the National Governors Association seemed to have been the first step in trying to pull together enough support within the state where not only governors but state ed leaders, regional ed leaders, a lot of people came together.

A former Gates staffer described how the initiative emerged under Sanford, as the small schools portfolio was beginning to fall out of favor:

> [Sanford] had a PhD in education with a focus on public policy, and when she came in, she said, "If we're going to change the debate publicly, then we've got to start to impact public policy." The strategy was, starting with the governors, we've got to build support at the state level, and once we build support at the state level, then when the dynamics are right (which would have been 2008), and we get an administration that has—more importantly an education secretary whose school district benefited from our support—then you've got the ability to drive forward and push it off balance at the federal level. Almost all the governors signed on, and then they started pushing the core standards that all states need to embrace a similar set of standards for graduation. When Obama came into office, you got Arne [Duncan], who says, "Yeah, they're right; we need to do this."

This multipronged strategy, which involved top officials at both the state and federal levels, was a linchpin in the foundation's success, as one interviewee described: "We put together a strategy that said 'Okay, while we focus on the federal public policy, where we really need to do our work is in the states.'" Thus, Gates made grants to a variety of state education leaders, including most notably the Council of Chief State School Officers, to support their work on common standards, generating support from a wide variety of influential officials. These successful results were unprecedented and surprising even to Gates employees themselves, as one former Gates official described:

I have been somewhat surprised by how far they got in this. It's been hugely successful. We got the national curriculum standards and that was amazing; I didn't think they would ever pull that off. I didn't think it was going to succeed; I thought what they were trying to do was impossible.

Gates's involvement in federal policy also became more concentrated as the foundation assumed a central role in the design, guidance, and implementation of major federal grant competitions such as the Race to the Top and Investing in Innovation funds. One Gates official described the foundation's role as an advisor to states on the use of federal funds in the following way:

We made consulting support available to states, technical assistance to help them. Potentially the Race to the Top winners [are] going to have a ton of money, but they don't necessarily know how to turn that into policy and practice change. So [we're] really trying to bring expertise to bear now to help make the states and locales make best use of the Race to the Top dollars and really have a sustained policy change. Because the potential, particularly in this fiscal environment, for that money to get poured on the ground [into] backfilling and whatnot, the pressure to do that is going to be really high. So how do we help them do better than that?

To address these concerns, Gates aimed to develop systems to ensure that classroom-level instruction was appropriately aligned with these policy changes at the district level. One Gates official explained this strategy:

We believe that part of the answer to that is not only the Common Core where you have a high-quality, clear, coherent set of standards but then a set of tools, assessments, aligned professional development, curriculum. So that it's really clear what teachers need to do, what kids need to know and be able to do, and then the great tools that are available for teachers to use them. How is it that we can help catalyze those tools for teachers so teachers are more clear on what they need to be doing?

By 2010, Gates's activity and centrality in both federal and state policy was striking, especially when compared to its early institutional reticence to engage in these contexts. Staff consistently described Gates's leaders as initially hesitant about policy influence as an education strategy since its founding in 2000, and deliberately avoided pursuing advocacy-related initiatives for the first several years of the foundation's existence. In its early years, Gates's Washington, DC, office was initially named the "East Coast" office so as to avoid any association with attempting to influence federal policy. As one former Gates staffer described: "They didn't want to call it the 'DC Office' because they were just putting their toes in the water of getting involved in advocacy."

Gates's tendency toward supporting policies that predominantly aligned with liberal politics also deterred advocacy activities in its early days, as one official recalled, "Our program people were like, 'No, no, no. That's all of that political stuff.' Particularly back in the day when people didn't like the Bush administration, all federal politics for people in Seattle looked like doing stuff with the Bush administration." One staffer echoed that a "very strong bias" against policy existed at Gates for its first eight years, noting that "It was much more legitimate to be involved with policy post 2008 with Obama."

From 2008 to 2012, the foundation's reticence toward policy influence diminished notably, as a former staffer explained: "They're in the mix and they're no longer terrified of what it means to engage in direct advocacy." Gates officials noted an "evolution," as one staffer described, as policy influence gained a more important role in its overall education strategy. One Gates official explained, "It evolved with respect to its place in the organizational food chain. Its change of status was ascendant and rapid. It's obvious that if your goal is ultimately the institutionalization of things that you demonstrate, then you need law, policy, and resources."

In 2008, Bill Gates left his position as CEO of Microsoft and began to work with the foundation full time. Several Gates staff noted that around this time, Bill and Melinda Gates began to realize that the foundation's work in both public health and education required more complex levers than grant making alone, and the couple began to view the foundation's role as a policy actor in its own right, as opposed to "simply writing checks," as one official described. As a family, Bill and Melinda Gates "started to think about how they can use the power of their voice to influence policy," according to one source. One former Gates staffer reflected:

> When [Bill and Melinda Gates] first started the foundation, there was a sense that the kinds of gifts that they were making, say, in the world of vaccines were so large and so much larger than the gifts anyone else was making that they would be able to affect significant change. [But] traditional grants, even very, very large ones given to really good entities, were not going to create the systemic change that they wanted to affect. So pretty quickly the foundation started to recognize its particular power in that regard with respect to both who the benefactor is and the size of the institution. Melinda [Gates] literally said that "We recognize that our philanthropy is just a drop in the bucket, and the size of the problems that we're taking on [is] really significant compared to our budget and even a foundation of this size cannot go it alone."

These internal shifts catalyzed significant changes in Gates's grant making. Overall, between 2005 and 2010, the proportion of Gates's education resources allocated to advocacy efforts more than quadrupled, and in 2009, it spent $78 million on advocacy, out of a total $373 million annual education budget. From 2010 to 2015, the foundation's spending on advocacy represented almost 20 percent of its education budget. A Gates official described this change as a strategy designed to produce significant return on investment:

> *What a dollar worth of program buys you versus a dollar worth of advocacy if it works—the potential leverage in terms of public dollars can be enormous. [The focus on advocacy] interpenetrate[s] a lot because we want to get maximum leverage out of the program investments that we make.*

Eli and Edythe Broad Foundation

The Broad Foundation was founded in 1999 in Los Angeles with a mission to "advance entrepreneurship for the public good in education, science and the arts." Its benefactor, Eli Broad, founded two businesses, KB Home and SunAmerica, which provided homebuilding and retirement savings services, respectively, and created the foundation after the sale of SunAmerica to AIG. Broad is the smallest of the four foundations studied, both in terms of its endowment size ($2.6 billion) and its staff, which is intentionally kept "lean," as sources shared. Its education work has focused on urban school districts with high levels of student poverty, and its grant-making criteria mandate that its investments must bear the potential to produce "transformative and catalytic change."

One Broad official stated that "the goal was always to influence or impact the system whether it was at the district level or state or national," while another staff member explained that the foundation purposefully targets areas that "others have ignored," noting that the foundation prefers to make grants in areas where "we as the Broad Foundation can come in and really try and have sort of a catalytic effect, and highlight something that has been off the agenda." Broad was founded with the explicit intention to apply Eli Broad's success as an entrepreneur to the charitable causes he supported, as the foundation's website described: "the Broads focused their charitable giving in a new style of investing that was more akin to their business acumen: venture philanthropy. An entrepreneur at heart, Eli Broad has applied his same spirit of creating new enterprises to the family's approach to philanthropy."

Throughout its history, Broad has consistently emphasized market-based reforms in its education investments, centering on the values of competition, efficiency, effectiveness, and accountability. These values are reflected in Broad's support for initiatives such as school choice and the development of high-quality charter schools through charter management organizations, along with financial incentives delivered through differential compensation structures for teachers and district leaders, also known as "pay for performance" or "merit pay." They also include developing human capital pipelines into teaching and district leadership by building alternative pathways to teacher certification and incentivizing managerial professionals to assume leadership positions in urban districts; plus restructuring district governance systems to improve accountability.

Broad's highest-profile efforts have involved the development of leadership pipelines, or strategies to increase the presence of managerial professionals within the education sector. Broad's pipeline programs are primarily administered through the Broad Center for the Management of School Systems, which manages two initiatives: the Broad Residency and the Broad Superintendents Academy. The Broad Residency is a two-year program that "places emerging, talented private sector leaders into full-time managerial positions" in urban school districts, with the intent of increasing efficiency and effectiveness in underperforming districts. As of 2012, the Broad Residency had placed two hundred residents in fifty school districts, charter school management organizations, and other education organizations since 2002.[8] The Broad Superintendents Academy maintained similar goals but facilitated the entry of established executives from high-level corporate backgrounds into education leadership, in contrast to developing a pipeline of younger managerial talent. The Academy funded a ten-month course for "experienced leaders from business, education, military, government, and nonprofit sectors with the critical skills needed to lead our nation's largest urban school districts," many of whom were then placed into superintendent positions with Broad's assistance. In 2012, Academy graduates served as superintendents or school district executives in fifty-three cities and twenty-eight states, and in 2009, Academy graduates were employed in 43 percent of all large urban superintendent positions. Broad also funded a number of other pipeline programs that aimed to increase the supply of managerial expertise in the education reform field. They included Education Pioneers, which placed graduate students from top universities into summer residencies and one-year fellowships with education reform organizations in major urban centers, and New Leaders for New Schools, which trained managerial leaders for principal positions.

Broad's support of pipelines was complemented by its investments in structural change in several urban districts, which resulted in the institution of several high-profile reform measures, particularly in the area of differential compensation. In 1999, Broad was a key player in a privately funded initiative in Denver, known as the Pay for Performance Pilot. The program was an experiment in providing bonuses for teachers who were considered "high performing" as measured by their students' achievement gains on standardized tests. After the pilot's four-year provisionary period ended, the Board of Education and members of the Denver's Classroom Teachers Association (the city's teacher union) approved its continuation as a broader model of teacher compensation, at which point the program became underwritten by public funds.

The pilot's success led to Broad's investments in other cities' plans for performance pay, including Houston, New York, and Washington, DC. Houston's superintendent, Abelardo Saavedra, participated in the Broad Superintendents Academy in 2002, and in New York, Broad provided the first year of funding for the city's merit pay pilot program (which was terminated in 2011 after studies showed that differential compensation had no effect on student achievement).[9] Notably, in 2008, Broad was central in developing a version of the Washington, DC, union's contract that piloted performance pay using a combination of value-added statistical measurements as well as peer assessments from experienced master teachers. Broad's merit pay pilots are predominantly located in cities where the foundation maintains close relationships with high-level education leaders through the Broad Residency, the Superintendents Academy, or other education reform allies. In Washington, DC, for example, Broad worked closely with then-superintendent Michelle Rhee, who exemplified Broad's interest in alternative-pathway investments as a former Teach for America teacher and founder of the New Teacher Project (and also starred in the 2009 documentary *Waiting for Superman*, which Broad partially funded).

In addition to merit pay initiatives, Broad has been a key player in restructuring efforts in New Orleans over the past ten years following Hurricane Katrina. One Broad official noted the foundation's role in instituting a new school system—one that is now 100 percent charter schools—as "something we're particularly proud of." This official characterized the current New Orleans as one of "significant performance that previously didn't exist, due to getting most incentives right through charter management organizations." One Broad official noted:

> *We've gone from a place where most schools are failing, and other schools are a C or a D—where no school is an A—to a place where every year has continuously improved. We've taken risks with a broken school system to build a dynamic improving school system. Students there have opportunities that they didn't before. The FBI was in the district because there was so much corruption, and those issues have just gone away. The system's not perfect, there are challenges, but it's a lot better off than it was before.*

Like Gates, Broad has also been a strong supporter of state standards, which dominated many of its policy-related efforts at the state level in 2014 and 2015. As one respondent noted: "The Common Core fight was a pretty significant bump last year. Conversations about it dominated to the exclusion of other priorities." Nonetheless, one Broad staff member believed, the "opt out had little impact and the center held"—meaning that backlash to the Common Core State Standards was not as widespread as some had feared. This respondent also noticed continued interest of top leaders in the education agenda that Broad endorsed, noting "The terrain is a little different, but the governor is still interested in education work, and the president and Secretary Duncan are still pushing forward on a strong agenda."

In 2012, Broad engaged in a major strategic planning process that resulted in a plan to more directly target policy change through what interviewees described as "transformative" federal and state policy investments. According to Broad interviewees, the strategy channeled approximately 40 to 50 percent of Broad's resources toward advancing policy-related efforts.

W. K. Kellogg Foundation

With a $7.3 billion endowment, Kellogg is the fifth largest foundation in the United States. In contrast to Gates and Broad, Kellogg originated in 1930 in Battle Creek, Michigan, with an endowment derived from an industrialist fortune in cereals. Kellogg's mission has centered on aiding vulnerable children, as the foundation's original name, the W. K. Kellogg Child Welfare Foundation, suggests. Its original intent, expressed in a document called the "Children's Charter," was to "help people help themselves," with an expressed goal to "help children face the future with confidence, with health, and with a strong-rooted security in the trust of this country and its institutions." The formal mission was revised in 2007 to the following: "The W. K. Kellogg Foundation supports children, families, and communities as they strengthen and create conditions that propel vulnerable children to achieve success as individuals and as contributors to the larger community and society."

For the first eighty years of its history, Kellogg's programs were organized into individual program areas, but the foundation has recently undergone a major reorganization into three broader areas: education and learning, health and well-being, and family economic security, or in foundation shorthand, "educated kids," "healthy kids," and "secure families." The overriding goal of these three program areas, or "themes," as several Kellogg staff members characterized them, was to target vulnerable families using an integrated lens to make program decisions as opposed to considering education and health as necessarily separate categories. Within the "educated kids" area, strategies such as "Whole Child Development" were designed to "support comprehensive and integrated approaches to healthy child development that strengthen the social, emotional, cognitive, physical, cultural and civic development of young children." The "healthy kids" area included a strategy described as "improve food systems by engaging local leaders in communities and schools (parents and other stakeholders) to deliver healthier foods to all children and achieve related policy changes." "Secure families" aimed to "organize community colleges to create stronger educational linkages between high schools and employers, while serving as a community resource and engagement center for low-income youth and families."

Thus, key goals related to education were targeted across multiple program areas. This reorganization was initiated with the intent to "break down silos" between individual program portfolios, as one Kellogg official described, in contrast to Kellogg's prior structure. As a result, staff worked together on cross-cutting initiatives that often included resources from multiple areas. For example, one major initiative involved the advancement of a "farm-to-school" model of providing healthy, local food to school districts, a strategy that encompassed resources from both the health and well-being and education and learning areas. One Kellogg staff member described the initiative in the following way:

> *What we want to do is build collective policy action across the foundation that leverages the collective. So what in our farm work can we leverage or use in our education or in our health? It's interesting; those have been sort of under-the-radar issues for many years, and now with the sort of revolution and awareness around food and childhood obesity, now school, farm-to-school issues, all of those . . . the coalitions we helped build, the school food focus, a whole network of big city school districts and looking at their school food programs.*

Another Kellogg staff member described the foundation's central role in elevating the status of breastfeeding in US culture, which was a primary strategy in the "healthy kids" area, and how this initiative linked to other foundation areas:

> [A] specific example is a foundation's commitment to create a breastfeeding nation. When we go to talk about food and obesity and changing the diet and improving the access to food and eliminating food deserts in the urban and rural settings, we know that we want to create conditions that change the eating habits of zero to fourteen [which starts with breastfeeding].

One Kellogg official related an anecdote that illustrates these depictions of Kellogg's organizational culture as cross-cutting in its topical approach:

> So Governor [Rick] Snyder, we met him shortly after he's elected, a group of philanthropies, and he says, "I'm adopting a P–20 approach to my work in Michigan." And he went on to say that's PreK to 20. So when we went around the room, I said, "Governor, I hope you consider changing the P to stand for prenatal rather than PreK because it starts at birth. Education starts at birth and all of these things that we're learning about healthy development of infants and toddlers . . ." [But] the early childhood world, the professionals in early childhood also don't link very much to the health-care providers. The systems of funding and programming in the early childhood space, zero to five, are fragmented, chaotic.

This official further described the process that the foundation engaged to integrate these varied streams into a cohesive, "interconnected" approach rather than a "siloed" one:

> We don't just come with an education and learning framework. We're saying, okay, what are the health services? How does Medicaid and SCHIP support that family? How does all the health

support then feed into the early cognitive development and the social emotional development? Is that a health issue? So you work to have more of a "whole child, whole parent" integrated approach across specialties, and then taking community engagement and community context seriously.

Several Kellogg staff members noted that while the new organizing framework was met with a positive reaction within the foundation, vestiges of the previous structure still remained. In prior years, "leveraging the collective" was not a priority and teams were "very competitive," as one Kellogg official described:

The foundation functioned more as a university where each faculty member has their own body of professional work and their classes. [Likewise] each program officer had their portfolio of work and they were the king or queen of that, and that's how we functioned.

Another staff member explained how the foundation was addressing this issue by integrating staff from backgrounds outside of the philanthropic field:

The culture here used to be the one with the biggest portfolio wins. And so if you started the big, huge, $7 million initiative and you were carrying that grant and the board knew your name, it was like, "Pshhhhhhh . . . I can kick my feet up." And . . . you're seeing this influx [into Kellogg] of sort of folks from nontraditional backgrounds, coming not from philanthropy [but often from policy backgrounds and nonprofits].

Informants often pointed to Kellogg's history as a primary factor in determining its decision making, consistent with empirical evidence that organizations are imprinted with norms characteristic of their founding time periods, and sustain these norms even as their external environments change.[10] Multiple Kellogg interviewees invoked the foundation's founding norms and subsequent history to explain why the foundation was active in policy:

I think that Kellogg has a lot of largesse because we're older. We have a history in certain things, and . . . we're invested in those things still. I think that the fact that we're sort of historically entrenched in certain things, and . . . we've groomed our board members to be a certain way . . . is what makes it that way.

Many interviewees discussed the influence of the Kellogg family's legacy in defining the organization's "DNA." As one staffer described:

It's part of our genetics, focusing on underlying policy infrastructure, since 1930, but in a subtle and understated way. It's a genetic part of our institutional work—it's part of our DNA here, the value that we give voice to those who are invisible and voiceless in policy conversations.

These values stemmed from the Kellogg family's political and religious history, according to Kellogg staff members. The Kellogg family followed the philosophy of Seventh-day Adventism, especially its focus on physical health. This value manifested in a philanthropic emphasis on health care for the vulnerable, inspired by a Kellogg child with special needs that could not access proper medical care following an accident. This interest in providing health care joined with the family's commitment to abolitionism and formed the basis of a progressive foundation that emphasized civil rights in low-income communities. One informant explained these values:

They were Adventists and abolitionists. During the Depression era, they changed the shifts at the cereal company to six hours so that more employees could work. They thought about their employees' work, families, values, health—they didn't want their wealth to be on the backs of poor people. That was their legacy as early as 1930, taking care of primary needs and pursuing racial equity.

These core values have remained deeply rooted at Kellogg. A number of interviewees quoted W. K. Kellogg's statements, such as "I'll invest my money in people," in describing how the foundation made grant decisions. These values translated to a long legacy of policy activism, according to staff members.

Ford Foundation

Ford, the second largest foundation in the United States, has an endowment of $12.4 billion, and similar to Kellogg, its wealth is rooted in an industrialist fortune: its original benefactor, Edsel Ford, was the son of Henry Ford, founder of Ford Motor Company. Also like Kellogg, Ford was founded in Michigan, where Ford Motor Company was headquartered in Dearborn, in 1936, but later moved to New York City in 1953. The Ford Foundation's original charter specified that its funds be used "to receive and administer funds for scientific, educational and charitable purposes, all for the public welfare," leading to a broad interpretation of mission, or as one Ford official described, "so broad you could drive a truck through it." Since the 1950s, Ford's board members determined that the foundation would work in the "most pressing areas" as opposed to selecting specific topical areas of focus, a distinctive model among the foundations studied. For the first eighty years of its existence, the foundation's key goals were stated as "strengthen democratic values; reduce poverty and injustice; promote international cooperation; advance human achievement." In 2015, under president Darren Walker, Ford's central strategy was revised to focus 100 percent of its resources on remedying social inequalities. One Ford staff member described the foundation's culture as centered around progressive causes and facilitating a structure to support "citizen action," in the same vein as Kellogg: "[Ford emphasizes] what I would call the basic infrastructure of citizen action in the United States and around the world . . . civil society groups, networks, alliances trying to make sure there was enough money for people to organize themselves for progressive causes."

These progressive causes were particularly visible in Ford's work during the 1960s and 1970s. A number of respondents noted, however, that Ford's most extensive and ultimately successful policy work in education was not in the visible and direct policy influence that Ford pursued in civil rights areas, but in the relatively unrecognized area of school finance reform. In the 1970s, Ford elected to challenge the tenets of school finance law that had resulted in disparities in school funding across districts and states. To do so, it assembled scholars from elite universities to develop empirical work on school finance equalization. In addition, Ford supported public interest law institutions with the intention of building litigation and practice to challenge existing inequities in state-level school funding. In the words of one respondent, "Ford is *the* foundation that led to finance equity in the United States."

Ford staff members spoke about the foundation's legacy in a similar manner to Kellogg, invoking the foundation's legacy and values, with particular attention to the foundation's assertive social justice stance that defined it in the 1960s and remained an important part of the foundation's institutional identity. One Ford official explained:

> *The policy work is basically part of everything we do. In addition to what happened in the '60s [with the civil rights movement], we have legacies around some of the issues that are part of the history of this institution. It's the entire program here. Everybody from the president on down is on the same page about that.*

Another Ford staff member confirmed this characterization about the foundation's "democratic, inclusive social justice work," and explained how it informed the foundation's decision to transition into inequality-focused work:

> *When we were thinking about our transition, we confirmed our values and our history in social justice, and doubled down on that. We're still in this process of looking at the inequality work and work on education more generally, continue with our core values of building capacity of communities to participate—building more agency and power, and offsetting efforts of elites and business leaders. Elites don't understand what policies will be best for*

communities that are underserved. It's a disconnect to have an education strategy that's market driven, that might drive away the creation of good schools in neighborhoods with low capacity.

According to several interviewees, Ford's focus on education diminished somewhat in the 1980s and 1990s as the foundation became more involved in international affairs and the rule of law and democracy. This change reflected Ford's institutional mandate on addressing the "most pressing problems" in society rather than committing to specific and consistent topical areas. From 2010 to 2015, Ford's education program focused on funding innovations related around the central theme of "redesigned and expanded learning time." It invested in initiatives that extended, reorganized, or lengthened the school year, aiming to increase instructional time, facilitate more avenues for higher-quality teacher professional development and collaboration, and engage low-income students in enrichment opportunities. One Ford official described this process in the following way:

If you could expand the school day and school year and use that as a lever to redesign the entire day for students and for teachers, you could support better teaching through time for collaborative work and the interaction of teachers and outside partners coming into a much more comprehensive program. . . . It would be a wedge, a lever into the system that could then get at these larger infrastructure problems.

In 2015, Ford announced that the entire foundation would be reorganized to address issues of inequality on a systemic level, a move that was widely heralded as transformative in the philanthropic sector as well as aligned with an increasing political focus on wealth disparities and systemic poverty.[11] One Ford official explained this process in the following way:

Historically, it's no surprise: inequality is our North Star. Not necessarily explicitly, but our grantees and core work have always been focused on groups of people that aren't included or are left behind economically, by globalization or urbanization in the US. Our core assumption involves the importance of agency of these communities—to realize the democratic ideal in the United States and emerging ideals in places like South America and South Africa— people have to be engaged.

In this context, respondents shared, Ford's prior emphasis on expanded learning time would continue but would no longer be a primary focus. As one staff member described the change:

We're trying to push it in as not a silver bullet, but as a cocktail of different interventions—as one of the levers for improving the capacity of schools to deliver how professionals work collaboratively.

Like Kellogg, Ford staff invoked the importance of policy influence as an almost taken-for-granted element of their work throughout their history. One informant described Ford's culture of policy, particularly as it related to social justice issues, as "unique and quite longstanding at the foundation." And similar to Broad, Ford's culture is up front and unapologetic about influencing policy as part of its mission of mobilizing marginalized populations and advancing social justice. All interviewees made statements that described the role of policy at Ford as central to all of the foundation's activities, noting that engaging in policy was an avenue that enabled the foundation to give voice to populations that are typically excluded from mainstream political processes. One interviewee explained:

We ... think that the voice of people most impacted by a policy, or a direction, should be part of the policy debate. So, often we would support advocates who would advocate from ... the perspective of Latinos in Texas, or ... sometimes we support youth because we want to have their voices heard in the policy debate. So [we're thinking about] advocacy and interest groups and, particularly at Ford, we're focused on marginalized communities. We want to make sure that those voices are part of the policy debate.

"Walking the Line" and Negotiating Legal Boundaries

While all four foundations considered policy influence as core to their organizational values, strategies, and identities, they varied distinctly in how they enact those values in the context of existing legal regulations, ranging from being overt and aggressive to "under the radar" in terms of their actions in the policy realm. While Gates is now an active policy funder, it was initially reticent about political involvement of any kind. Over the fifteen years of its existence, it has embraced policy influence as a central strategy yet remains highly cautious about legal regulations. In contrast, Kellogg has been highly committed to policy influence throughout its nearly ninety-year history yet has also been cautious about the ramifications of its activities, similar to Gates. Until the past five years, it has predominantly operated behind the scenes, reluctant to engage its own brand publicly as a visible advocate and preferring to advance its goals through its grantees' activities. Conversely, Broad and Ford have both viewed policy influence as a central priority since their earliest days of existence. They maintain organizational identities as active and visible policy actors, yet express these identities in significantly different ways.

Gates: "Walk Right Up to the Line"

Gates's significant investments in policy-related strategies and its increasing acknowledgment of its own power as a brand were carefully managed to remain in full compliance with legal restrictions. As living benefactors, Bill and Melinda Gates played an instrumental role in setting the tone for the foundation's policy engagement over time. Recalling instructions from Bill Gates himself, one respondent noted: "What [our benefactor] would say is, 'I want you to walk right up to that line. Don't cross it. Don't ever cross it, but I want to walk right up to it.'" To facilitate "walking right up to the line," Gates developed a series of institutional safeguards to stay within legal boundaries. One Gates staff member described "internal policies about a legal vet for anything that goes to a government office," noting, "We're very conservative about that." Gates also instituted an entire department staffed by officials who were specifically trained about advocacy-related issues, effectively acting as "traffic cops" to ensure that the foundation's efforts in policy were "scrupulous" in terms of not crossing the line, in the words of one official. This role involved not only training staff members and managing portfolios of policy-related activities but also managing relationships with relevant policy actors. As one staff member described:

> Our advocacy folks get involved—who talks to the governor when and with what message and how often. It's their task to be a part of certain meetings, to know what's going on whenever anybody is going to be talking to certain government officials in a given state or in Washington, DC, and just help to guide, direct, and make and shape and also keep legitimate any activity that crosses the line into [lobbying].

Foundation officials engaged in substantial due diligence to guarantee that grants were "clean," as one interviewee described. To vet and advise grantees, Gates staff were well versed in the intricacies of anti-lobbying restrictions; as one policy officer noted, "I still stand firmly, no grant I did crossed any legal lines; that I walked right up to the line." One program officer at Gates described a culture that bordered on "micromanaging" the policy-related aspects: "We would have ongoing conversations about particular grants. Like could a grantee do this with our dollars? Or could a grantee not do this with our dollars?" Similarly, another former Gates staffer shared:

> I will say we also would talk to grantees about [the boundaries], about walking up to the line. If you have three funders providing a third of your funding each, and your lobbying activities are 20 percent of all of your activities, as long as they weren't directly funded solely by one of the funders but they were funded through all of those funds or through multiple funders, then it could be funded.

So we would talk to grantees about that. You had to be very clear in how you talked about it.

Aligning with Gates's increasing comfort with engaging its own institutional political capital, Gates staff consciously used their own personal and professional relationships to advance advocacy interests, as well as leverage the prestigious Gates brand to lend legitimacy to its initiatives and activities. One person described the following scenario:

So I would, for example, meet with the speaker of the house in [a state] and we would just share thoughts on issues. This is a good example of where our legal training came into play—as long we weren't talking about issues that were currently being discussed as legislation, we could talk about anything. So we talked once with the speaker of the house who wanted to do higher ed reform, and we just shared some ideas on that. We would talk about charter school quality with him. He was one of the state's big charter advocates. I'd go to dinner with the senate education committee chair and we'd talk about college-ready graduation requirements, before there was any . . . core legislation, and she was a member of the P16 council. So we would use our personal influence that came from being affiliated with the Gates Foundation, and there is an enormous amount of power and influence that comes with having your name affiliated with the foundation.

Broad: "Putting Its Neck Out"

Broad represents the most aggressive and least apologetic foundation of the four, presenting its goals openly and pursuing them vigorously. Broad generally engages in activities that "hug the line," in the words of a staff member, to a greater extent than peer foundations: "We're probably more aggressive in terms of policy and advocacy than other organizations and other foundations." Another echoed, "[The] foundation doesn't have a problem getting into contentious issues and doesn't have a problem putting its neck out there a little bit." For this reason, staff commented that finding partners with "the same worldview" and "desire for dramatic change" was difficult at times, and that Broad generally does not engage in coalitions of funders for this reason, with the exception of partnerships with Gates and a handful of others on specific initiatives. One Broad official referenced an example of a hands-off strategy that Broad would not consider pursuing:

> It's not just about doing good research; it's about doing good research and putting it together in a way that's going to have impact. As you know, there is no shortage of white papers in education.

In fact, Broad interviewees recalled that the foundation's approach toward policy was so explicit that other foundations were uncomfortable with some of Broad's direct tactics. In describing this dynamic, one Broad official attributed the foundation's assertiveness principally to the influence of Eli Broad:

> [Broad staff members] were constantly getting pushback by people at Gates because their in-house counsel felt sometimes the activities weren't appropriate, and I think we are a little bit more willing to be on the edge of that—just because that's how Mr. Broad is— and if we went to him with some of the issues that Gates was having a problem with, he wouldn't care about it. He just would want them to resolve it and then see how we could move forward.

The role of policy influence at Broad has taken on an even more central position in the foundation's strategy the past several years, wherein Broad has aimed to award as much as half of the foundation's annual education grants to policy-related activities at state and federal levels. One official summarized this change:

> Generally speaking in the past, our policy making has been important, but in terms of our involvement in a lot of things but not in terms of our investment. It's been about 10 to 15 percent. We're looking at trying to do somewhere between 40 and 50 percent of our investments going forward in the policy realm.

Perhaps most illustrative of its assertive approach to policy influence, Broad established a sister organization under section 501(c)4 of the tax code to complement the 501(c)3 foundation's work. A 501(c)4 organization has fewer tax advantages and fewer lobbying-related legal regulations than a 501(c)3 foundation, including the ability to engage the services of lobbyists to promote political issues, which private foundations cannot. One Broad staffer described the 501(c)4 as a central element in enabling Broad's evolving strategy:

> The mix that [our benefactor] has currently working for the foundation helps us be much more strategic. Our business plan is going to focus on our number one priority, [which] is policy. Now would we be able to hold ourselves accountable for that if we didn't have C4 money available to us to be able to do that?

As Broad staff disclosed, however, the two organizations are not entirely separate from one another, by design. Several foundation employees are paid, in part, by funds from the 501(c)4. One noted that "[Our benefactor] funds a portion of [direct advocacy work] privately [through a C4]." Another described the payroll structure: "In addition to the foundation, [our benefactor has] been able to provide a few of us with payroll off of [the benefactor's] private family office. Which is a C4. So some of us are actually part time on a C4 and also part time on a C3 salary." This structure is legal, and in practice not uncommon among private philanthropists. However, few are as open as Broad in acknowledging this strategy, which informants described as a feature of Broad's culture, as mandated by Broad as benefactor, to unapologetically use the full spectrum of resources available to advance its goals and impact.

Kellogg: "We Don't Put Ourselves Out There"

Although Kellogg invested in a number of policy-related initiatives, it remained relatively guarded about its public image with regard to policy and political issues, an approach that one informant described as "under the radar":

The foundation does a lot of policy work that's very aggressive. We're very active actors in DC. We have a history of doing things here, but we do it under the radar. We're pretty conservative.

One respondent described how the foundation was cautious about its reputation: "We're in the middle of an identity project to really put our reputation out there a little bit. We're a large foundation, but we don't put ourselves [out there]." This staff member compared the foundation's actions to Gates: "Gates has been so strong with getting out there, and using their own branding and their own name." Another Kellogg informant described this ethos:

So policy used to be a real dirty word, and you're better off calling it anything but policy still. Some people chalk this up to being a Midwestern value—we want to be sort of a silent partner, and we don't want to step out and put ourselves out there and take credit for anything, and we feel like if we get into policy that we're going to have to do that.

The informant further contrasted Kellogg's approach to other foundations' more visible strategies:

As opposed to somebody like a Gates—ed reform, ed reform, ed reform. But that's highly politically charged. They're making friends and they're making enemies—no question about it. I don't think that we like to do that. If you look at our grant making in terms of public policy, we like to water it down. We like to be one of thirty partners on a federal initiative where we don't get too dirty, and we don't really say too much.

One interviewee described this dynamic in the following way:

As soon as you start talking about changing public policy and public priorities, not surprisingly, you are in the middle of very hotly contested, emotionally charged, and frequently mean-spirited back and forth. A lot of corporations or individuals that get into

philanthropy are just trying to be good citizens, and they'd rather
go somewhere where people will say, "Hey, thank you. That's ter-
rific," rather than somewhere where they're going to be eviscerated
as the domineering bully boy. And so giving to scholarship funds
or giving computers or giving money for curriculum materials—it
will only get people to say nice things about you.

Several staff members at Kellogg expressed personal ambivalence
about the ongoing changes, as one source stated: "[Senior manage-
ment] was intentional about saying, 'We're coming into a different
phase.'" Interviewees relayed that Kellogg's board had experienced tension between members who sought to engage actively in policy and
those who were wary of overstepping their bounds. One respondent
described, "Philanthropy is accountable in many ways to the boards of
directors, and there's a variety of levels of comfort with policy influencing, advocacy, and the political spectrum. . . . You've got diversity on
your board; you've got . . . the extreme Republican Tea Party guy, and
then you've got the flaming liberal." Another staffer echoed this concern: "Our board meetings are generally two days, and one day you'll
have the same person say, 'Yes, we should be doing advocacy,' and the
next person saying, 'No, we shouldn't be doing that.'" Staff explained
that some board members were particularly aware of political polar-
ization around controversial topics and were concerned about retaining the legitimacy and prestige of the foundation. As one respondent
explained: "I think that's sort of a thing for the foundation. I mean, they
don't necessarily want to step out in front of something and get burned
for it. At the same time, they want to maintain credibility." Another
elaborated on this statement:

I think that what [the board] might be a little afraid of is if, for
example, . . . they took a stand on something, that it would polit-
icize essentially what they're trying to do, and they don't believe
it would necessarily be an effective means of getting to that end.
It's like you've got this ideology, and policy is a potential lever to

pull to operationalize that ideology. But they're also scared that if they pull the lever . . . what's going to come out is more than just the outcome.

Thus, staff members attributed board members' uncertainty to the risk of being associated with controversial topics, accompanied by a fear of legal or public backlash. One official described, "The more high profile you come out as supportive of policy, I mean . . . the more at risk you place yourself." Another described the board's general attitude in the following way:

They don't necessarily want to step out in front of something and get burned for it. I think that there are some on the board that would really like to do more policy work but also understand that there's a double-edged sword that could really come back and bite us. There are others that really want to stay away from it. Every now and then the radiator gets too hot for us, and either senior management or more often the trustees say, "Oops, you're going too fast!" or, "Oops, that's a little bit too much!" The risk aversion comes up.

Kellogg interviewees also invoked the concept of "walking the line," similar to Gates officials. Rather than describing a willingness to approach it closely, however, they expressed discomfort with the ambiguity of the definition of "policy work" and wanted to avoid the appearance of lobbying. As one source described: "It still seems like that . . . gray 'no man's land.' . . . It's pretty scary over there. You've got to be really careful or you'll get too close to the line. As you get close to the boundary, it's more sensational." Interestingly, however, Kellogg staff members were generally less concerned about legal censure and more about reputational sanctions—the threat of "public outcry," as one interviewee noted, as opposed to residual threats of the Tax Reform Act, which was not seen as a serious issue. A long-term staff member described this dynamic in the following way:

In the '90s, there was extreme paranoia about the word "lobby." We were mostly worried [about] criticism from the public. For a while we were uptight about the legal, but we spent a ton of money and did a lot of reconnoitering and all of that, and we are much more comfortable on the legal front. We managed the hell out of that. But as you know, there aren't that many legal constraints. This is a pretty big hole to drive through, right? It's really not that constraining. It's more about the public opinion, sniff test.

In 2013, the culture at Kellogg began to change significantly, both among the board and the staff, with regard to willingness to engage in policy. One informant related a key moment that turned the board, following a presentation by an education advocacy group that Kellogg funded:

The willingness of people [at Kellogg] to engage in the policy space has changed, and the key turning point was two or two and a half years ago [in 2012]. We brought in Kati Haycock from Ed Trust [a leading advocacy organization in K–12 education] who presented disaggregated data that had been tracked over time, showing how multiple [racial and socioeconomic] groups were performing on education metrics and showing state and federal investments in education. In that meeting you could see among the trustees that the light bulb went on that we need to be engaged and involved in this policy issue, that this actually matters. Previously to the board, policy had equaled politics, and politics is problematic. But the quantitative representation and data points showed that the policy side of this matters directly to the outcomes, especially for kids of color. They saw they had a role to play. So policy shifted from a dirty word to something we openly talk about.

Ford: "It's the Whole Program Here"

While more reminiscent of Kellogg in its emphasis on social justice, Ford more closely resembled Broad in its similarly open and assertive embrace of policy influence as a key organizational pillar. Ford had an upfront and assertive approach to public policy since the 1960s, as evidenced by its central role in the Tax Reform Act hearings of 1969. One interviewee, who had worked as a program officer at the foundation during this period, described how the foundation's policy activities began to become more overt under McGeorge Bundy as president:

> *In the '60s, Ford embarked on an aggressive set of programs that definitely interacted with public policy constructs. It tried to push public policy around, tried to create public policy, and had previous experience trying to do it mainly passively through creating national commissions or giving money to White House commissions or stuff like that, and then McGeorge Bundy came to be president of the Ford Foundation when he left the Johnson Administration [where] Ford had already pioneered some interventions called the Gray Areas project.*

The activist identity that Ford adopted under Bundy persisted over the next forty years. Staff pointed to the foundation's history of active out-front policy advocacy, noting that this did not change after the 1969 Tax Reform Act, despite Ford's censure in Congress. One respondent described the transparency of Ford's strategies for influencing public policy, noting that the foundation was careful to remain "clean" in terms of the Tax Reform Act:

> *Was [a specific initiative] an attempt to influence public policy? Absolutely. Did we know in advance what public policies we wanted to influence? Yes. Did we know in advance what the ground rules were of the Tax Reform Act? Absolutely. We had an in-house general counsel and a staff of five other lawyers. [The restrictions] didn't chill in any way the selection of a program arena. It didn't chill the definition of the problem. It didn't chill the strategies. Were the strategies developed in ways that were legal? Yes. Were we aware of the restrictions? Yes. Did we have to work around a few of them? Yes.*

Ford interviewees were by and large reflective about the legal restrictions that constrained their actions, elaborating on the informal strategies the foundation could "safely" use to influence policy. For example, one respondent described knowledge building and educating the public as "safe strategies":

> So what are the approaches to doing this? There's knowledge building, supporting research that just basically builds a deeper understanding. So knowledge building is clearly a strategy and it's a safe strategy. Then there's another sort of strategy around building public will, and that led to support for books, support for movies, support for convenings.

Others acknowledged that their social justice goals sometimes entered into murky territory. One respondent described,

> I'm pretty clear in my mind that there's a line in the sand that foundations shouldn't cross and that those are legally defined, and also defined in terms of what I would call good foundation practice which would be recognized by most of my peers. But I also realize that's a slightly abstract solution to the real problem, which is that people want to use their money for political purposes and they will get around the rules if they can. I have to say there are probably a couple of occasions in [the] Ford Foundation when I was there when I crossed the line. I think that's just being honest.

A Nuanced Spectrum of Involvement

Thus, the four foundations' relationships to policy work are nuanced and dynamic, rather than monolithic. In the following chapters, I examine how these differences manifest in the foundations' management decisions with regard to policy and introduce a framework for conceptualizing the distinct approaches these foundations pursue.

3

"There Are Basically Two Kinds of Foundations"

Conceptualizing Foundations' Policy Involvement

The distinct differences between foundations' approaches to policy work are rooted in fundamental contrasts in their institutional norms and values. One former Ford staff member described these contrasts as "fault lines," commenting:

> I think there are now more clearly drawn lines within and between foundations where different philosophies are clashing, and that's interesting theoretically as well as practically. I feel I'm in the middle of more of a battlefield ideologically. I would say only in the last five years has that come about.

Another interviewee, a philanthropic consultant, corroborated this statement, arguing, "There are basically two kinds of foundations." A Gates grantee summarized the difference between foundations he had worked with in the following way:

> *One group of funders are highly strategic, top-down, technocratic, and have clear policy goals that they're trying to move, as evidenced by Gates or Broad. Then you've got a slew of foundations who have a more decentralized approach. They have a set of values that they believe in and they give unrestricted general operating support to advocacy and community-organizing groups that generally share their values and are moving an agenda. And they don't exactly know what's [going to happen]; it's not like the foundation decides "This is the housing agenda and here's how we're gonna move it." They say, "Hey, here's a bunch of groups working on housing that generally share our values; let's give them money and see what happens."*

The four foundations' approaches to policy are more complex than this characterization might indicate; however, I argue that they can broadly be located along a spectrum of two contrasting modes of engagement, defined by four interrelated and mutually reinforcing institutional norms:

- How do the foundations manage grantees?
- How do the foundations select partners?
- How do the foundations frame problems?
- How do the foundations evaluate results?

These norms are presented in Figure 3.1, which represents the core conceptual framework for the next three chapters.

At one end of the spectrum, foundations aim primarily to attain desired policy change and produce impact, and policy involvement thus represents a means to an end of institutionalizing reforms. I describe this end of the spectrum as *outcome-oriented*. By "outcome-oriented,"

FIGURE 3.1   Outcome-oriented versus field-oriented approaches

Outcome-oriented approach	Managing grantees		Field-oriented approach
	Centralized ■ Control of an initiative is maintained by the foundation	**Decentralized** ■ Foundation delegates more control to grantee organizations	
	Selecting partners		
	Grasstops ■ Foundations prefer to work with elite and/or expert organizations	**Grassroots** ■ Foundations prefer to work with community-based organizations	
	Framing problems		
	Technical ■ Foundations pursue problems that are amenable to technical solutions with a clear line of causality	**Adaptive** ■ Foundations pursue problems that are complex and multifaceted with less clear solutions	
	Evaluating results		
	Quantifiable ■ Foundations prefer metrics that are calculable and prove impact	**Integrated** ■ Foundations use both qualitative and quantitative metrics to show plausibility rather than proof	

I refer to efforts to achieve goals that are determined at the outset of an initiative and measured by indicators that grantees are held accountable to. At the other end, foundations prioritize the democratic engagement of citizens over the achievement of specific policy outcomes. I describe this end of the spectrum as *field-oriented*. By "field-oriented," I refer to efforts to build, support, or transform existing or new organizational fields through investing in organizations' capacities to pursue social change over a long time period.[1]

Gates and Broad both predominantly align with the outcome-oriented end of the spectrum, with some variance. They often view policy engagement as a lever to efficiently direct their resources toward desired policy outcomes, framing their decisions with the question: "How can philanthropic funds be invested to produce the greatest return on investment in the most effective way and with the most efficient use of time?" Both foundations are driven by a "tremendous sense of urgency," as one Broad interviewee described, and a desire to generate outcomes that produce significant change, as described by multiple Gates and Broad staff, who used the words *transformative, game-changing*, and *major impact* in describing their goals. Given this sense of urgency and need for swift action, Gates and Broad interviewees reported that the foundations often viewed democratic governance as a hindrance or obstacle to achieving impact, preferring instead to manage their initiatives using an elite, expert-driven agenda to foster innovation and agility both in program design and implementation.

In contrast, Kellogg and Ford are primarily on the field-oriented end of this spectrum. As a first-order priority, they value the democratic engagement of broad populations in decision-making processes as opposed to focusing on efficient and effective outcomes. They frame their decisions using the question: "How can philanthropic funds be invested to build the capacity of a field in order to develop sustainable solutions?" Kellogg and Ford informants both tended to view their foundations' roles as "infrastructure developers, facilitators of debates, and conveners of people," as one Ford staff member described, as opposed to Gates's and Broad's comfort with using their institutions' own brands and political capital as tools to pursue influence. One Ford official described this distinction as a "support versus control" function, wherein a "support function" entailed the foundation acting as a convener and facilitator and allowing those in the field to "work it out on their own," versus a "control function," which involved a higher degree of hands-on management and monitoring from foundation officials.

An outcome-oriented approach aligns with the concept of "strategic philanthropy," an approach toward foundation management that originated in the late 1990s.[2] Strategic philanthropy, also sometimes referred to as "venture philanthropy," emphasized results-driven management practices and the targeting of resources toward a determined point of impact.[3] A strategic philanthropic approach is based on a "theory of change," or a core set of assumptions about a series of processes, initiatives, and practices that follow a chain of logic to guide a foundation toward predetermined goals, which are measured by concrete indicators. This approach emerged in the 1990s as a reaction to what the new foundation managers viewed as "traditional philanthropy," or the older foundations that utilized hands-off, laissez-faire measurement and evaluation practices.[4]

In the field of education, strategic philanthropists embraced what Sievers describes as a "market-inspired stance that views school systems as aspiring to the model of corporate enterprises."[5] This market-inspired stance emphasizes managerial values and producing measurable impact, as Sievers notes:

> *The language of the field increasingly reflects this orientation: investments (rather than grants), value-chain, scaling up, impact, branding, performance metrics, bottom-line, measurable outcomes, theory of change, entrepreneurship, logic model, market segment, benchmarking, reengineering, and similar terms drawn from the scientific and business worlds.*[6]

The policy initiatives of particular interest to strategic philanthropists within education included the development of common curricula and national academic standards, high-stakes accountability through standardized testing, differential compensation (also known as "pay for performance") for teachers, and charter schools, or publicly funded, privately managed schools intended to induce competition for public schools to improve. In particular, strategic philanthropists have funded networks of branded charter schools, known as charter management organizations (CMOs), which are designed to grow the charter school movement to produce catalytic impact across a wider population of students.[7] The growth of CMOs has been largely fueled by a handful of foundations, including Gates, Broad, Robertson, Dell, and the NewSchools Venture Fund. In fact, from 1998 to 2005, CMOs received 90 percent of philanthropic funding to charter schools in California, despite enrolling 10 percent of students.[8]

This emphasis on catalytic impact is often described as an "entrepreneurial" mindset, or what many philanthropists refer to as a "high growth, high impact" approach.[9] One interviewee described the "entrepreneurial wing" of the field philanthropy, expressed by foundations that value competition, accountability, and standardization, as manifested through support of charter schools, state standards, and teacher quality:

> Gates, Broad, Walton, the NewSchools Venture Fund have become very big funders of a lot of the entrepreneurial [reforms] . . . these are the new players. I do think there's been this tendency to identify reform as charters; it's market-based solutions and it's holding teachers more directly accountable for student learning and anything else is status quo. The entrepreneurial wing of the movement including some of the funders have managed to help sell this.

Strategic philanthropists are also notable for their interest in engaging directly in policy contexts in order to produce greater return on their investments and leveraging and amplifying their grant dollars—again, representing an explicit contrast with traditional philanthropy.[10] According to Scott, this "high engagement" approach is rooted in a desire to maintain quality through the use of management techniques learned in business contexts: "They often believe that educational reform could greatly benefit from the strategies and principles that contributed to their financial successes in the private sector."[11]

POLICY AS A LEVERAGE TOOL:
A MEANS VERSUS AN END

Interestingly, across all four foundations—not just Gates and Broad—the concept of "creating leverage" was invoked as justification for engaging in policy-related activities. While sharing an interest in the same outcome, interviewees characterized the underlying norms that motivated these justifications differently. Interviewees from Gates and Broad described policy influence primarily as a means to an end, or a tool to more efficiently leverage their resources toward achieving outcomes. In contrast, Kellogg and Ford respondents described policy influence as an end in and of itself, a way to build grassroots coalitions and to increase the democratic mobilization of the communities that they targeted. These two contrasting ways of looking at policy work—as a means to an end versus a means in and of itself—were raised in conversations with numerous interviewees.

Informants at all four foundations compared philanthropic resources with governmental allocations to education, arguing that foundation funding is miniscule relative to the state—by one estimate, Bill Gates and Warren Buffett would have to give away their entire fortunes thirty times over to compare to Andrew Carnegie's and John D. Rockefeller's contributions proportional to government spending in their respective eras.[12] Interviewees from Gates and Broad consistently highlighted this ratio in their description of their interest in policy engagement, often using managerial terms such as a desire to produce "return on investment" and "bang for the buck." Reflecting the power of a metaphor, a number of Gates and Broad respondents independently cited Jay Greene's chapter in Rick Hess's 2005 volume on education philanthropy as a seminal work that helped inspire both foundations' interest in policy advocacy as a "high leverage" strategy.[13] Greene described the impact of educational philanthropy as "throwing buckets into the sea," representing just $1.5 billion of annual funding in the context of a $427 billion public school budget, and argued that investments in policy could help foundations amplify their funds' otherwise limited impact. This argument appealed to many actors in the education reform field, according to one respondent, a professor who taught both MBA and education students:

Jay Greene's piece is the piece that the students all immediately gravitate to, and it's seductive to think that investing in building new schools is a "high leverage" strategy, whereas investing in building the capacity of people in the mainstream system to marginally improve what they do is a "low leverage" strategy.

One Gates staff member directly cited Greene's argument, stating that Gates's funding accounted for one-third of the $1.5 billion annual education philanthropy in the United States, which in turn paled in contrast to the $500 billion public education budget:

[Greene's] argument says that if you [want to pursue] high-leverage philanthropy, that actually rather than taking your little bucket of money and throwing it into the sea, you ought to use your bucket to dig tributaries and have them impact the way that the public system and the public money works. Politicians decide how money flows, and public money is what supports these schools.

Likewise, Kellogg and Ford informants also described policy-related investments as a tool to magnify the impact of funds that would otherwise be insignificant in the context of government resources. A former Ford official described this rationale:

More and more foundations are emphasizing policy and de-emphasizing capacity building through the universities and the education of scholars, graduate students, professors. [That] style [of grant making] is increasingly harder for them to hold onto because it's less of a dollar-for-dollar efficient investment than investing in policy. In the fiscal crisis for education, it means that philanthropic dollars are much more highly sought after, in demand, and are capable then of more leverage.

A Kellogg staff member also made this argument, using the example of the foundation's work in its home state:

Depending on where the endowment is, our programmatic budget could fund Michigan state government for three days and Detroit Public Schools for three months. So the fact that these [issues have so] much effect on policy decisions determines our constituent base. It just doesn't make sense not to engage in policy.

Another Kellogg staff member elaborated on this argument, noting that influencing policy was the best way that the foundation could provide impact outside of directly providing social services that were the appropriate responsibility of the government:

That lever of policy work is even more necessary because we cannot get into the business of picking up direct services. For foundations it's an easy trap to get into, and policy helps their money go a lot further. It really gets this multiplier effect because if you don't do it, the money just [has no effect]. Three hundred fifty million dollars across [forty million vulnerable children] is just nothing—it's three or four dollars a kid.

Similarly, one Ford official described how foundation staff viewed policy influence as a "multiplier" for the foundation's relatively limited dollars:

The only way to have an impact across a broad group of people, particularly if you're not going to do what, let's say, Walton does, and try to fund every charter school in the United States, you have to think about, strategically, what are the issues and what kinds of policies [are relevant]?

A Ford official echoed this statement, emphasizing how important the foundation believed policy involvement was to achieve scale for its initiatives beyond local contexts and thus achieve systemic change:

So policy is critical across Ford in all of our areas because it's a way to promote some kind of impact at scale. I would say, in general, anything we do in the whole foundation anywhere in the world, we're trying to make systemic change; we're really trying to have long-term, sustainable, systemic kind of impact. If we don't work on policy, then we're really not able to [do that].

LEVERAGING POLICY AS
A MEANS VERSUS AN END

When asked why scale and leverage were important, informants from Kellogg and Ford used different language than Gates and Broad, despite having the same goals. Kellogg staff, for example, argued that leverage meant the foundation could "be as inclusive as possible," could support "processes of participation in communities" and facilitate opportunities to "support things that get more people involved." One official described Kellogg's approach toward policy as driven by the funded organizations themselves:

> *[Policy influence] is how you're going to really move that lever more broadly, but if you do that in a vacuum that's not well informed by people at the community level, then you end up with something that's probably more your ideas than it is theirs.*

One Kellogg official emphasized Kellogg's role in policy as facilitating connections between grassroots community efforts and institutionalized channels:

> *[I want to] develop processes for doing that [policy] work—not so much structures. I'm not as interested in saying, "Well, Kellogg needs to be the one to go in and help write the bill that gets this put into statute." Since we are good at people building, we can aim some of our efforts towards connecting communities of practice to state- and community-level advocates, to try to build a stronger link. The frame that I'm suggesting is one where we don't really do anything on the policy front, but we invest in people to pursue [the work] in their states who have credibility and some gusto and are kind of "up and comers" to do that kind of work.*

Similarly, Ford informants also referred to policy as a tool to enhance their activities such as "empowerment of people" and the development of "long-term, sustainable, systemic kind of impact." One Ford official noted, "We're really focused on addressing poverty and marginalization and inequity and all of that, [and] you can't address any of those things without dealing with the policies." Another staff member echoed:

> [Our] mission has to do with improving the lives and life chances of the most marginalized and disadvantaged people in society, and Ford has some very strong norms about how it does that, including one that says the people who are living closest to the problems and are most negatively affected by the problems should be centrally engaged in helping to develop solutions to those problems. So there's always at Ford the sense that there has to be a bottom-up approach to this.

Ford:
bottom-up

"SOLUTIONISM" AND MANAGERIAL EXPERTISE

These differences in the foundations' language regarding engaging in policy-related work are reflections of contrasts between the institutional norms and valued expertise that comprise their organizational cultures. In contrast to Kellogg and Ford, Gates and Broad reflected the resonant market-based values that characterized the nonprofit sector in the late 1990s and early 2000s, when they were founded.[14] Interviewees described Gates and Broad as having a "very business-oriented perception," as one described, primarily staffed by professional managers with expertise in strategic business planning techniques and quantifiable metrics to gauge impact.[15]

Several respondents pointed to the influence of Bill Gates and Eli Broad themselves as living benefactors, infusing practices and norms rooted in their corporate backgrounds into their foundation cultures. One interviewee, a consultant, described this as follows: "A big difference is whether the rich guy who the foundation is named after is dead or is living. They're just not the same; they don't think the same way." One Broad staff member reflected that whereas deceased founders were not physically present to exert authority or dispatch a sense of urgency, living benefactors like Mr. Broad tended to be more hands-on. One interviewee, an independent researcher, described Gates and Broad as former corporate CEOs who led hierarchical organizations and who were "accustomed to being able to say, 'We're going north!'"

While Bill Gates and Eli Broad are often categorized together in the media as "new philanthropists," however, their approaches differ substantively in terms of their professional orientations, with Gates representing a new-era economy that focused on technology, and Broad representing a more traditional approach that emphasized training the proper employees with the appropriate substantive expertise. One interviewee, a professor, aptly summarized this nuanced distinction:

> *Eli Broad and Bill Gates are these two very powerful, very successful businesspeople, but one [is from] the old economy. I think of Eli as a nineteenth-century captain of industry type, and Gates is a techie. They each bring this very powerful sense of what it takes to actually build successful organizations. For Eli, it's all about getting the right people into leadership positions, and Gates, I think at bottom, he sees the problem as mostly a data problem, as you might expect.*

This comment underscores an important difference between Bill Gates and Eli Broad as benefactors and, by extension, between their foundations' cultures. As a product of technology wealth and breakneck technical innovation, Gates valued data-driven empiricism as a means to solve entrenched problems, both corporate and social. This "technocratic consciousness," in the words of Habermas,[16] is distinct from a typically managerial focus on effectiveness and efficiency.[17] Rather, a technocratic approach, which Morozov describes as "solutionism," focuses on engineering solutions to problems.[18] Silicon Valley scion Sean Parker describes this ethos as "a desire to 'hack' complex problems using elegant technological and social solutions, and an almost religious belief in the power of data to aid in solving those problems."[19]

This technocratic solutionism, prevalent at Gates, has more recently begun to characterize peer foundations borne of twenty-first-century Silicon Valley wealth, Parker's among them. As one Kellogg official observed, "We have seen some change in philanthropy that's been driven by technology, and these new mindsets around what philanthropy might mean." One former Gates staff member described Gates's culture as "dynamic, strategic, entrepreneurial—there's an 'all in' mentality—an engineering mentality. Engineers are problem solvers—they look for bottlenecks and efficiencies."

This "almost religious belief" in technology as a lever for social problems contrasted distinctly with core institutional norms at the older foundations, Kellogg and Ford. Interviewees pointed to how Kellogg and Ford were organized around professional cultures that they described as "academic" in nature. Until recently, these foundations' presidents historically came from prior professional backgrounds in the academy, as one Ford official stated:

Traditionally, many of the presidents and leadership at the major foundations came from the academy. They had very similar norms that look a lot like the norms of a university. [They make grants to organizations] that meet certain academic standards for the production of their work—they have internal review; they hire people with PhDs.

According to this interviewee, foundation leaders who were primarily socialized as scholars took a "rational" or "hands-off" approach toward policy:

They very much believed that you put as much intellectual capital and put it in the system and the policy makers will then be able to take that up and make the best decisions possible. They just strongly believe that if you can get the best studies, the best information, that's the most powerful way to affect policy, and so you invest in building the capacity of the smartest people you can find.

Another respondent agreed, noting that foundation leaders from the academy made investments in research and analysis with the expectation that "people will take more enlightened actions based on this knowledge." Interviewees shared that shifts toward the legitimacy of managerial expertise began in the 1980s, as foundations began to become interested in more direct and measurable ways of intervening in policy, as opposed to relying on the agency of intermediaries to take up rigorous social science knowledge. One informant described this in the following way:

> I think that there was an expectation that if they supported the research or if they supported demonstration programs that it would just be automatically picked up by government and that information alone would sort of drive policy decisions, and that's not just the way the world works.

This quote aligns with a statement from one Kellogg staff member, who noted that the foundation had debated whether or not Kellogg's traditionally hands-off approach had produced the momentum on the ground that the foundation desired. One Kellogg official described the situation as follows:

> I think how people expect that this good information will sort of diffuse into the populace and laws will change. I think that it's been hit or miss. In some places, we've seen really good work and good traction. I think in other places, we have not.

This approach recalls historical accounts of foundations' investments in intellectual capital building rooted in behavioral and social science disciplines, which were traditionally viewed as the most rigorous sources for developing expertise that could be brought to bear on informing policy decisions.[20] In contrast, the first several decades at the "new foundations" were generally led not by academics, but by managers trained in business, rather than social science or humanities. One former Ford official commented, "The chief [influentials] are coming from business schools, and it's a different set of tools than the people who come from academia [in the social and behavioral sciences]." This official further described this development as a "revolution" within philanthropy, commenting:

Economists have overshadowed sociology and anthropology as having made a case that their tools are more useful for studying a variety of social problems. And so with that comes a different mode of analysis and a different entry point.

As valued expertise within foundations has changed, so has the substance of strategies aimed toward addressing social problems, a shift reminiscent of the Progressive Era's changing center of gravity from charitable services to scientific philanthropy. Some identified the transition to a more managerial approach as a beneficial one, since it facilitated the development of more effectively functioning organizations:

[The older foundations are] largely staffed by academics, former university presidents, and deans. That's a particular form of organization, it's very atomistic, they don't bring people up. Our department chair did nothing to help me learn the ropes. I walked in and they handed me a $12 million portfolio, and I got more orientation on my health benefits than I did on foundations. It was just "go do."

The rise of managerial expertise as a dominant point of view has caused contestation within some foundations. One interviewee, a former Gates official, commented on the substantive clash of norms between strategic managers and staff with academic backgrounds: "[Our new foundation leader who was an MBA] wasn't familiar with public policy." Meanwhile, a Ford official explained:

As you bring in more and more people who are trained in strategy, their approach to policy is very different. They see policy as something that is only marginally touched at the margin by information or even capacity. They ask the question, where can we provide money that's going to really move the policy quickly and efficiently?

This question bears a core thread of an outcome-oriented approach: "How can philanthropic funds be invested to produce the greatest return on investment in the most effective way and in the most efficient use of time?" In contrast, the question from a field-oriented perspective might instead be, "How can philanthropic funds be invested to build the capacity of a field in order to develop sustainable solutions?" This distinct difference forms the core of the following chapter.

4

"How Do You Establish a Bottom-Up Versus Top-Down Mix?"

Managing Grantees and Selecting Partners

The four foundations contrasted significantly in their styles of managing grantees as well as the types of organizations they preferred to fund. Whereas Gates and Broad retained control of their policy-related efforts centrally at the foundation level, Kellogg and Ford managed their efforts more loosely at the foundation level, giving decentralized substantive decision-making control to grantees (see Figure 4.1).[1] Additionally, Gates and Broad tended to predominantly work with elite and expert groups, such as elected officials or high-level influential policy players, whereas Kellogg and Ford focused on engaging and mobilizing the communities they targeted in addition to targeting elites.

FIGURE 4.1   Managing grantees: Centralized versus decentralized

	Centralized	Decentralized	
Outcome-oriented approach	▪ Foundation retains strategic oversight of grantees, who are held accountable to negotiated outcomes	▪ Foundation delegates control and direction predominantly to grantee organizations	**Field-oriented approach**
	Gates Broad	Kellogg Ford	

MANAGING GRANTEES: CENTRALIZED CONTROL

Both Gates and Broad exercised control over the direction of their policy priorities, determining what organizations would be funded to fulfill specific expectations. They also held grantees accountable to outcomes that were expressed as concrete deliverables, often worked out in negotiation with the grantees prior to awarding grants. One respondent, a professor who had worked with both foundations, paraphrased his perception of how Gates and Broad approached grantee management in their policy initiatives: "We'll hire [grantees] the way you'd hire a contractor, and we will specify exactly what we want from them." One Gates grantee commented on this dynamic in the following way:

> I have a couple of [Gates] program officers, and I think they wish they were doing this work—that is, being the policy person. There are significant causal arrows going in the direction from what the program officer wants to [what we do]. It's a nuanced relationship between funder and grantee, of course—we're not automatons, and it's their goals balanced with ours—but there are incredible causal arrows.

A Gates staffer described this approach, wherein the funder takes a "high engagement" mindset in managing the day-in, day-out work of grantees, as "[doing our] damndest to do whatever it takes to get that done"—consistent with the foundation's cultural value on urgency.

Similarly, another Gates informant described how the foundation took an active approach to designing and executing its strategy, rather than operating indirectly through grantees:

They're not just willing to write checks to organizations that have a proven track record of dealing with a particular issue that's of importance to the foundation. They're interested in figuring out, What are all the things that we can do? What are all of the tools that we have in our toolkit that can really help us solve this damn problem? We've tried downstream approaches. We want to go upstream and figure out how to stop this.

One Gates grantee described how this "upstream" approach manifested in its relationship with the foundation:

We've been funded by Gates for over a decade to do specific projects. We don't ever submit an unsolicited application to them. A lot of times we'll talk about specific things we can do and how it contributes to their bigger goals, and we [shape those ideas] pretty heavily in terms of what the specific activities they want to see and fund. A lot of times at the activity level, the Gates applications are enormous, but by the time we're filling them out, we've had all the conversations and it's a formality.

A Broad staff member made a similar comment, describing the agreements that grantees were held accountable to:

We have our terms that we use when we put an agreement together [and they] are generally viewed in the field as being more comprehensive. Others would say "micromanaging." It depends on your perspective, but we think they're more comprehensive than what you see from most foundations. I've seen some sets of terms from foundations that are two pages. Ours generally are ten.

A grantee who was funded by both Gates and Broad further commented on the high level of due diligence, specificity of negotiated contract material, and engagement from the foundations' program officers:

> *Gates and Broad program officers are engaged. They are all quite activist, doing a lot of framing, telling us more what they want out of something. The program officer pushes a specific goal or activity. They do a lot of homework and due diligence. They're orchestrating across several organizations to achieve a goal, and we're one part of that community, where we have specific things that we can deliver and advocate for. [By contrast, other] funders say "Here's the money, here's some general goals, this project sounds good."*

Gates and Broad informants described these high-engagement practices as a way to ensure quality control and professionalism in terms of the initiatives they funded, as opposed to ceding some control through more laissez-faire management practices. One Gates official explained that delegating greater responsibility to grantees might result in lower-quality initiatives that would then be associated with the foundation's name; these initiatives then would represent a liability. The official described the foundation's reluctance to delegate control to grantees rather than maintain centralized control, aligning with the archetype of the "hands-on" foundation:

> *It's a trickier game when you do it that way because there's certain limits to the degree to which one can manage a grant once it's made. When you grant it out, you lose a certain degree of control. It just means a lot of extra work up front defining what that grantee will do, but it also amplifies whatever message you're trying to send and it brands it as owned by the organizations you funded rather than by the foundation. It lends a certain kind of "source credibility."*

A Broad staff member echoed this statement, evidencing the foundation's careful management and protection of its brand:

We have had projects that we've done where we've pulled our names off of them, basically saying, "We've funded it, but you guys go ahead and do what you want to do with it." It just doesn't fit our quality bar, and so we're not going to be associated publicly with the project going forward because [if it's not] going to make the right difference, we're not going to attach our names to it.

MANAGING GRANTEES:
DECENTRALIZED CONTROL

Kellogg's and Ford's approaches to managing their policy-related initiatives exemplified a more decentralized approach. Staff members at both foundations described processes that purposefully devolved control away from foundation staff and toward grantees who were "reasonably self-directed," as one Ford official stated. The two foundations, particularly Ford, preferred to give general operating support grants as opposed to delineating activities directly or holding grantees accountable to discrete, specific outcomes. Respondents tended to view their role as "support[ing] the broader processes of democratic problem solving in society by building capacity," as one described. A former Ford official, reflecting on his tenure at the foundation, described this approach as the following:

I knew that I was not going to do what almost every other foundation program officer likes to do, which is come up with the answer and go around and sell it to [grantees]. This is philanthropy in 95 percent of the cases of major national philanthropic initiatives. I said, "We will never say what the correct program is ever."

Another former Ford official agreed, stating:

Ford would never do that, and it would simply say, "It's very important that these issues are raised. It's very important these conversations are had, and it's our role to foster, facilitate, and support them, but we're not going to pretend that we have the answer and push you in one direction."

This interviewee framed Ford's goal as trying to "create a stronger container" for deliberative debate to occur in the public arena, in order to gain "broad popular support in the long term" and institutionalize social reforms instead of "directing people to do this or that or say this and that." Another Ford staff member echoed, "[We hire] people who came with a more democratic spirit, if you like, for grant making, and who never saw their role as very aggressively promoting one policy over another."

One Ford staff member described the foundation's current thinking about "pivoting" its work from a focus on extended learning time to a focus on inequality as a means of illustrating how the foundation approached problem solving around strategic issues it wanted to pursue. It placed an emphasis on allowing its grantees to maintain their own goals outside the foundation's direction:

> *By giving core operating support, we allow organizations that are doing the current work to pivot without negotiating with us and [allow] new coalitions to develop.*

Similar to Ford, Kellogg informants also described a decentralized approach toward grantee management, explicitly underlining the foundation's mission of community engagement as central to how the foundation managed its policy efforts:

> *[Here's] a textbook [example] of how the foundation, with its tradition, would work: The momentum starts with the people, and they came to you. You didn't go to them and say, "Hey, I have an idea for how we can do this." They came to you and you say, "Okay, how can we give you the tools so you can fully realize [your goals] and use a democratic system?"*

Another Kellogg staff member related an example of a policy innovation in a state that had emerged from a local program without foundation intervention:

What I think gets missed is that some of the best policies that we've been able to influence have actually come from just good programming. [This] program grew to a point now where it's part of a larger initiative [and] gets state-level funding to do that program everywhere with all sorts of kids. Nobody ever thought that like from the outset, "Oh, yeah, we're going to make a policy change here." It happened [organically].

Informants from Kellogg and Ford often used the language of the "rights" of foundations as policy actors, questioning their legitimacy to intervene in policy contexts without broadly generated input. For example, a Ford official explained:

We're [not] the source of all wisdom inside the foundation. Who gives us the right to organize anything in a really precise way? We're really not part of the polity. We're not elected officials and we're not funded publicly. So I think there's a tension around that is unresolved. I think that's the biggest problem.

Likewise, Kellogg informants noted that they preferred to relinquish tight strategic control of grantees' work, preferring to determine more general policy goals and delegate authority to grantees to make decisions about contextually appropriate tactics. One staff member explained, "The viewpoint is that our good work will stand on its own enough to a point that people will notice and want to make the necessary changes in government that sort of show that these things work." A Kellogg official described the foundation's primary policy strategy as attempting to "empower" communities rather than underscoring the foundation's own institutional priorities:

We're enabling people to become involved; we're linking them to resources and opportunities; we're helping them build that capacity and then catalyzing them to continue to work so it's sustainable over the long run. We can bring resources and points of view and expertise to bear, but it's the community that builds its own public will.

Kellogg informants underlined the foundation's policy efforts as reflective of its core identity as a "community-focused" organization, one that emphasized the agency of grassroots communities, democratic processes of organizing, and civic engagement. One respondent explained:

> *Whose capacity are we building? We're doing this for the community, we're doing this for the most vulnerable, we're doing this for children, for families who are totally lacking and do not participate in economic systems.*

Another Kellogg official made a similar statement:

> *The way we do work, and what we do, is responsive to the people. We're building the capacity of their voice. We're doing policy with the community, and we're always taking the long picture. We want community voices solving their own problems. We do community governance. The grantees speak for themselves.*

Managing Grantees: Use of Brand and Political Capital as Institutions

Kellogg and Ford staff members reflected on their perceptions of their own power and ability to influence policy through their brands and political capital. These perceptions contrasted with those of Gates and Broad, where respondents described being assertive about using their legitimacy and prestige directly, rather than operating primarily as a broker and convener of grantees. Aligning with a desire to move policy processes quickly and effectively, Gates and Broad respondents referenced their foundations' own "voices" as visible public entities with the ability to direct attention to and confer legitimacy upon their policy priorities. One Gates staff member described this dynamic in the following way: "Because the Gates foundation saw itself as an actor, it would be very closely [involved with its initiatives] to ensure that its overall initiative goals were being met."

Interviewees cited the presence of living benefactors as a key factor in Gates's and Broad's comfort levels with direct policy engagement. One source, a professor, described this engagement as follows: "Foundations with living founders or donors—Broad, Gates—find it easier to leap into some of these conflictual reform efforts." Likewise, another respondent, a consultant, invoked the shorter history of these foundations, which were not concerned with preserving a century-old legacy:

> In old foundations' headquarters, they're not interested in shaking things up too much or endorse a controversial policy. Good money, good job. There's not much of an incentive if you're in that situation to end up in the minority or in a big fight where you might lose.

As such, the hands-on involvement of the Gates and Broad families in their foundations enabled their staff to stand behind their benefactors' names and credibility, as well as having confidence in the directives they received. Several interviewees described a charge from Bill Gates in 2008 to leverage the foundation's reputation toward its end goals, as one former Gates staff member recalled: "[Bill Gates said to] 'Use our influence as much as we use our philanthropy.'" Similarly, Broad officials cited Eli Broad's personal interest in leveraging assets toward realizing policy outcomes as a key factor in determining the foundation's assertive organizational culture, noting that Broad had viewed policy influence as a core element of his desired strategy since the foundation's inception. One Broad official explained:

> [Our benefactor] had always known that the operating environment in which schools function was a barrier to seeing some of the reforms happen that we initially had started out focusing on as a foundation, and so he really felt like if we could focus on the larger picture by removing policy barriers, that that would probably be the best way to leverage his dollars.

At Kellogg, however, staff and board members expressed a variety of conflicting opinions about how much the foundation should engage its political capital under its own name, as opposed to primarily enabling grantees to advocate. One informant related:

The theory before was to communicate our work through what the grantees were doing. Now, what we want to do is get our name out there more for the purpose of influence. There's places that we can do or that we can navigate that some of our grantees can't.

Another respondent explained how some at Kellogg sought to realign the foundation's activism with its external reputation: "There's a whole move to being more aggressive. [Previously] we did a lot of things behind the scenes. The policy work that we did was very discreet, so I think that's changed. Now we're much more overt about it." This development, however, was debated within the foundation, as some staff members viewed a more active and visible role as antithetical to Kellogg's core values and culture and its emphasis on community priorities as opposed to strategic direction by the foundation. For example, one Kellogg respondent reflected:

[Some think] if we're going to do policy, we need to be at the table as one of the advocates saying, "Do this, not that." And that's not our role. I mean, that's the role of a lot of other organizations, but it's not really our role. We could fund organizations to do that, but it's not ours specifically.

Another Kellogg staff member echoed this statement, arguing that engaging community actors was Kellogg's primary concern, as opposed to being a visible actor with a strategic approach:

It grates me to see any other way [than a community engagement approach], but I also believe that there are people that can inform us about navigating the public policy arena, and how to formulate and be strategic. So I don't exclude them, but I know that their role may be different.

One source, a former government employee who worked with Kellogg on an education initiative, illustrated how Kellogg's conservativeness and discomfort with being "out there" with its name and brand had manifested during one event at the White House, a rare public policy–related event for the foundation. The source described how the Kellogg staff representatives were concerned about the message the event might send, which publicized its work on a controversial policy topic regarding the role of families and communities in early childhood education:

> They were micromanaging the details, and you could tell they were not used to [this context]. The invite list took a month to finalize—there was extensive vetting. The White House team wanted to invite people who disagreed, and Kellogg got so mad when they found out that [two dissenting people] were invited—it was not part of the message they wanted to advance. They clearly had a lot of concerns about their explicit involvement at the government level.

In contrast to Kellogg, Ford interviewees were very comfortable with exercising the foundation's own agency and legitimacy as a brand, similarly to Gates and Broad, but introduced important qualifications that aligned more with Kellogg's concerns. One Ford official stated:

> Often foundations lose that understanding of what their particular role should be. I think we're uniquely positioned in the [nonprofit] space to create institutions, to support people, to support ideas and, again, I think if you go beyond that and try to be too instrumental, [you're in trouble].

Another Ford official explained that Ford had historically faced criticism about its over-involvement in an international policy context, and that those lessons informed its current work in education and its use of its own political capital:

> [In the 1960s] Ford was accused of meddling in population control in India, and there's a direct parallel there to what's going on in the education field now. The foundation thought it knew the answer, and because it had money, it thought it had a right to intervene. But it had no right apart from being useful to other people who were more directly and democratically involved in the struggle.

SELECTING PARTNERS:
GRASSROOTS VERSUS GRASSTOPS

While Gates and Broad tended to target elites, such as elected officials and other high-level influentials, Kellogg and Ford emphasized
the civic engagement of broad populations. Multiple interviewees
described the distinction between these two strategies as "grasstops"
versus "grassroots" (see Figure 4.2). Marris and Rein describe this contrast in approaches as "top-down" or "bottom-up" in nature, wherein
top-down approaches support elite organizations and policy experts,
and bottom-up approaches focus on advocacy and community involvement.[2] As opposed to the more widely known concept of "grassroots"
mobilization of a broad base of constituents, one Ford interviewee
explained a "grasstops" approach as one that assumes "that what really
moves people are ideas that are directly relevant to the interests of powerful [people] and organizations that can move policy, and that everything follows that."

Grasstops Strategies

Both Gates and Broad tended to invest in what informants termed
"grasstops" strategies, working predominantly with elites in government to move policy objectives on shorter timelines than the state
bureaucracy would normally allow. One source explained: "What Gates
and Broad have done—their first order of business was leveraging at the
highest level the people who had the highest influence." One Gates staff

FIGURE 4.2   Selecting partners: Grassroots versus grasstops

Outcome-oriented approach	Grasstops	Grassroots	Field-oriented approach
	• Foundations prefer to work predominantly with community-based organizations	• Foundations prefer to work predominantly with elite and/or expert organizations	
	Gates Broad	Kellogg	
		Ford	

member described this process as "really target[ing] the key influentials in the state." Their strategies were similar in some ways, but Gates focused primarily on gaining the support of high-level influencers at the state and federal level, while Broad directed more attention to urban district leaders. One informant described Gates's strategy as

> Way grasstops. Their strategy was [to] find the five, six, ten people who matter the absolute most and target them—bring them on board and then find the other five who are likely to oppose you if you don't bring them on board and work with them, and that's how they did it.

Several interviewees recalled Gates's presence at the National Governors Association in 2008 as the debut, in effect, of its grasstops strategy. At this convening, Gates appealed to state governors to voluntarily join a compact around adopting common state standards, which proved to be an effective strategy, according to one source: "The National Governors Association seemed to have been the first step—that to me was where they began—they had started to think about how can we use the power of our voice to influence policy." Another source described how, as a key part of its Common Core strategy, Gates enlisted national advocacy coalitions to advance the goals it was simultaneously pursuing through the National Governors Association: "They gave the CCSSO [Council of Chief State School Officers] a big bag of money to work the politics with the governors along with the providers, which was achieved and quickly moved the policy."

Gates's cultivation of relationships with elites extended beyond local and state contexts and into the federal government. Several interviewees cited the appointment of President Obama's Secretary of Education, Arne Duncan, former superintendent of the Chicago Public Schools, as a turning point. The reason was that Duncan's staff appointments were often either former Gates officials or former Gates grantees. One respondent noted, "Once Obama was elected, I mean, Gates literally had people sitting at the Department of Education both formally and informally." These officials included Jim Shelton, Assistant Deputy Secretary for Innovation and Improvement and former Program Director for the Education program at Gates, and Joanne Weiss, director of the Race to the Top competition and a former partner at the NewSchools Venture Fund, a major Gates grantee that served as an intermediary funder for charter school management organizations. With President Obama in office, federal staff engaged current Gates officials in key discussions of importance regarding education priorities. As one respondent explained:

> *It gives you a notion of where the field is moving, because they have regular sessions or phone conversations between funders and the Department of Education officials including [Secretary] Duncan and including [Undersecretary] Jim Shelton.*

Another respondent, a professor and former Ford grantee, jokingly related an anecdote: "A counsel for the education department came to talk about administrative policy. At one point he slipped and said 'The Gates Administration.' He really did! Everybody just fell on the floor." A Gates official explained further: "The support that the foundation gave to the department either directly or indirectly, both financially and through intermediaries, greatly affected how some of the early Obama education initiatives were formulated and implemented."

Interestingly, while pursuing its "way grasstops" strategy, Gates recently began to incorporate more grassroots advocacy in its strategy. Interviewees noted that this development had evolved as part of Gates's broader evolution toward an interest in systemic reform, and its recognition of the role of advocacy groups and politics in social change, as opposed to a focus primarily on elites as leverage points. Allan Golston, president of Gates's US grant-making program, noted in the *New York Times*, "We've learned that school-level investments aren't enough to drive systemic changes. The importance of advocacy has gotten clearer and clearer."[3] One former Gates staff member described the impetus behind this change:

There is a big push right now to figure out how the foundation can engage more effectively and regularly with civil rights groups. The foundation has tried to reach out to the civil rights community with some success, but is now trying to be much more deliberate because I think they know they've got to work with organizations that are representing minority communities.

One former Gates official corroborated this claim, reflecting that Gates had traditionally had a "lack of putting grant seekers in the center of their theory of change" and maintaining "sensitivity to grantees as partners over time." However, the source continued, "Gates is now beginning to speak a different language," arguing that the foundation is attempting to become more responsive to its grantees and relationships with communities.

Although Gates has consumed the lion's share of press attention regarding its activities at the federal level, Broad was also a key player. Broad officials were closely involved in the process of working with the Department of Education. From Broad's perspective, informants described the deliberate "alignment" of Broad's agenda with the federal government's in a similar manner to Gates:

So on the federal level, there's a couple of things that we think are important. One is doing things that can educate policy makers and other opinion leaders about the importance of certain items on the administration's agenda. Things around, for example, national standards, differentiated compensation for educators, expanded learning time, growing the number of high-quality public charter schools. All things that we think are important, all things that the administration thinks [are] important as well. And so it gives us a unique opportunity to align what we believe is important for education change and taking advantage of the environment that exists.

Another Broad official noted the comparable priorities of Broad and the Department of Education:

We have in this administration a Secretary of Education focused on the issues that Mr. Broad has been pushing through the foundation for the last decade—more [instructional] time, quality of charter schools, the ESEA [Elementary and Secondary Education Act] authorization that looks at effective teaching, the current standards, common assessments, those are all things that the Broad Foundation had been working on for the first ten years of the foundation.

The Broad Foundation's 2010 Annual Report also described this alignment:

In many ways, we feel the stars have finally aligned. With an agenda that echoes our decade of investments—charter schools, performance pay for teachers, accountability, expanded learning time and national standards—the Obama administration is poised to cultivate and bring to fruition the seeds we and other reformers have planted.

Broad was also involved in restructuring initiatives in large urban school districts that were accountable to a single actor, such as a mayor, governor, or superintendent, as opposed to elected school boards. In 2006, Eli Broad reflected on his interest in school districts controlled by mayors: "In other cities, those with mayoral control—Chicago, New York City, Boston—things are happening from the top-down. . . . And they've made great progress in all those cities."[4] A central plank of Broad's policy work involved training managerial professionals to assume superintendencies or high-level management positions in districts through the Broad Residency. This work also involved cultivating relationships and supporting many superintendents in urban school districts and, in some cases, paying the salaries of high-level administrators and strategy consultants, such as an influential strategy officer in the Los Angeles Unified School District, and the district emergency financial manager in the Detroit Public Schools. One respondent relayed:

Broad [will] go to the superintendent at LA and say, "I'm going to pay the full-time freight for your strategy officer." And she could say, "You know what? There's all this controversy about the principal of a very popular school," [and Broad will respond] "I will pay for that principal—take it off your books, but I get to determine who you hire."

Grassroots Strategies

Like Gates and Broad, Kellogg and Ford sought to engage high-level policy elites in their initiatives. However, they primarily emphasized grassroots community organizing and cultivating political mobilization, particularly at Kellogg, which framed this approach as core to the foundation's institutional identity. One Kellogg staff member described how he engaged in significant on-the-ground constituent dialogue before feeling comfortable with making decisions related to policy efforts:

[We would be] sitting down with parents. "Okay, mom. What's the reality for you in this particular situation?" and literally getting to that level of intersection was critical.

Several Kellogg officials shared stories about instances in which other funders they had worked with had behaved in a paternalistic manner, without understanding the dynamics of grantees and organizations on the ground. One source described how Kellogg sought to diverge from those practices:

There's a variety of things going on [that Kellogg is pursuing] that are really impactful, but they came from the ground up. I think for a large foundation trying to do place-based community work, that has to be our conduit. If we try to be top-down, we're sort of biting our nose to spite our face at the same time that we're saying, "Here, community, we want to uplift you so you can do wonderful things."

Another Kellogg staff member echoed:

We try very hard to not do things to community but to do things with community, and I think that that might be another reason why we sort of stay back from the policy stuff because we feel like once we get into that space where we're going to be doing things to people versus with people. I feel like whatever the solution is, it needs to be people driven and investing in people to do that work, and developing people to do that work, I think is critical.

A third Kellogg official corroborated this assertion, describing the foundation's value on maintaining the "authenticity" of its grantees' priorities:

If there's a policy direction that grows out of [our work], then it's come all the way through the bottom and the top, and it's pretty genuine to what the people want, and it's different than us saying, "I'm a real wealthy guy who is well intended. And I want to change this. I want to open up twenty of these centers just everywhere because I've got the money to do it."

One official described a similar scenario, recommending that foundations should be careful about managing policy initiatives in a top-down fashion, for fear of being seen as irrelevant or arrogant in indigenous communities:

Because you have a DC organization that comes into the pueblo in New Mexico and they don't know what they're doing, yet they're talking about "Well, the Buffett investment in preK has. . ." and literally it's just sink or swim at that point.

Despite this institutional value on bottom-up engagement, Kellogg recently began to more purposefully integrate more top-down strategies through the development of a coherent policy agenda and strategic communications plan across the foundation. This change is in line with its broader shift toward more deliberately attempting to directly engage its own institutional political capital. Kellogg restructured its communications department to be less "ad hoc," as one informant said, and more of a centralized resource to help convey a policy-related strategy. Until recently, the foundation had not articulated a distinct vision around the type of policy actions that it engages in. One Kellogg official described, "We definitely have a history of policy activity at the foundation [but] don't have [a policy agenda]. It has ebbed and flowed over the years." This statement is in line with another interviewee's statement: "We don't choose an area of work around policy—policy flows through our work." Another respondent recalled how policy engagement was decentralized and exercised at the discretion of program officers, rather than as part of an institutional strategic plan:

You got $20, $30, $40, $50 million to go off and do an initiative, and [you] would have ten or twelve grantees that would be [your] body of work. It wasn't necessarily a bad model but didn't add up to a policy agenda. How does everything we do come together?

One source explained how the foundation was approaching the process of developing a policy agenda:

The policy agenda isn't fully developed yet, but the idea would be it's embedded in all the programming work but it somehow is coherent. I think that would be a first in the time I've been here. It was not as integrated [before].

This process was somewhat contested in the foundation, however, given its history and culture of delegating strategic decisions to grantees, and its deep commitment to avoiding policy for policy's sake. Staff members debated how policy "targets," or strategic goals, should be formulated, as one noted:

Developing a policy agenda and developing policy targets, for us, is also understanding, "How do we do that?" Do we develop loose targets and ... [let them] bubble up [from] our grantees? What they think are targets? [Do we] incorporate those, or do we get very tight targets and find partners to work with? Our value would be more the former, where we keep loose targets [that are set] by our

*grantees because of our [historical focus on] civic and community
engagement.*

Several Kellogg interviewees echoed this idea, emphasizing that
these processes of centralization needed to be managed with attention
to community engagement and stakeholder input. One described the
process of developing policy goals with sensitivity to "context that is
guided by the work" but also using the agenda-development process
as an opportunity to "be more efficient and being more organized, and
leveraging the collective." Another commented on the challenge of
maintaining this delicate balance:

> *This bottom-up approach to policy making, it has a lot of value but
> all of that formula, that intellectual theorem right there, is easier
> said than done. It's just a hell of a lot easier said than done. Policy
> making is not always steeped in data and common sense and ratio-
> nal logic but emotion and politics and romanticism.*

Interviewees described Kellogg's efforts to introduce a "common
language" around policy work. As one explained: "We want to develop
common-base language around policy. There's different levels of understanding what it is, and if we just can get on the same level . . ." Another
stated, "There's not really consistent language. Then everyone talks differently about what policy is. And most people affiliate policy with just
legislative action, law making." Staff members also invoked the foundation's self-conception and institutional tradition as an important element to retain during the process of becoming more strategic, and the
need to consciously focus on Kellogg's "humility" as an organization.
One interviewee related:

> *One of the pillars of our identity work is building accountable rela-
> tionships of the policy work. [In the past] we've been looked at as a
> very transactional funder, not being a collaborator, not being at the
> table. [We want to remember] the power and humility dynamic,
> knowing that we are at the table because our endowment is $7.2*

billion. Our value is we are a "besider"—we're not an insider, we're not an outsider, we're a besider.

While describing this community-centric culture as important to Kellogg as an institution, staff also reflected on a need to become more strategic as an organization. One source described that one of the detriments of being a "value-driven foundation" was that the emphasis on democratic inclusion in processes of decision making sometimes happened at the expense of accomplishing goals. One official described:

I think that's one of the issues of Kellogg is that we're such a value-driven organization that we don't quite get to actionable agendas. When we get to those agenda discussions, we drown it in value sets. That's a hindrance, and it also creates a fuzziness around really explicit, proactive, strategic action.

Over the past decade, the foundation had slowly been considering its strategic role as a policy actor and was taking more concrete steps to formalize it, as one source expressed:

We constantly think about it. We truly believe that we, from the bottom up, can create models and relevant experiments and lessons that have great value to be scaled vis-à-vis policy. We've got a lot of cool stuff we're doing that is model building for policy change. We don't quite have it packaged yet right; it's not completely formalized, and our rhetoric is still far from our practice. That's a critical institutional step I think we need to take.

Both Grassroots and Grasstops

Falling between Gates and Broad and Kellogg on the spectrum, Ford evidenced a mix of approaches that included elements both "grassroots" and "grasstops" in nature. Ford staff members described their program as a strategically designed combination of "bottom-up" values, akin to Kellogg's, with a "top-down" component more reminiscent of Gates's and Broad's approaches. One official described this combination in the following way:

As philanthropy over the last decade has gotten much more focused and strategic on policy change, we've developed a blend of strategy that looks both from the bottom-up but also works quite closely with those at the top who have considerable power to create the space, especially if people from the bottom are putting the pressure on to create spaces. So there's this bottom-up, top-down approach. We do work directly with elites as well.

Another Ford official used similar language:

You have to build the demand at the grassroots level, and then you had to build capacity at the administrative level to get things done as opposed to just going to the top—going to the governors and going to the state superintendents and getting them on board— [this idea of] "Let's just go to the top and work there" although obviously we do some of that—we work with the United Nations, we work with leaders of other countries, we work with people in the White House and those kinds of things. So the top-down, grass- tops approach is more of a Gates approach, and the Ford approach is both. It's bottom-up and top-down—grasstops and grass[roots].

In the context of its education work specifically, Ford informants also described another dimension within the grassroots/grasstops distinction, evidencing a strategic emphasis on "insiders and outsiders." The insiders represent teacher unions and established educational actors, and the outsiders represent newer reform-oriented challengers. One Ford official described this dimension of the strategy:

We believe very strongly that if you're working for policies that could be perceived as advantaging the marginalized over the already privileged, it's very unlikely that an insider-only strategy will do that. Institutions typically don't change in antimajoritarian ways voluntarily.

Examples of "outsider" strategies involved funding "powerful ideas and evidence" from researchers and public intellectuals, according to one Ford respondent, as well as cultivating advocacy groups and members of communities that schools served. This strategy is reflective of an emphasis on facilitating democratic debate, as a Ford official related:

> *We really believe we need to have an army of activists, includ[ing] members of the communities that need to have more equitable schools partly for democratic reasons. For the mission of the foundation, they absolutely have to be involved. Their local knowledge has to be mixed with expert knowledge in order to get a solution that really is decent and democratic for neighborhoods.*

The value-driven nature of this focus on deliberative democratic principles did not preclude an accompanying rationale based on strategic concerns, however, as the official elaborated:

> *We also think for sustainability and scale, [it won't work] if you don't have local communities really strongly advocating to get something adopted in the first place. And then, to make sure it sticks, because the local communities are going to be there over the long haul. With the turnover in school administration, in school board members, in mayors, and teachers, we think the two stable groups are really the teachers' union and the community members, and they have to be really involved. That's [. . .] very much an outsider and bottom-up kind of strategy.*

By contrast, an example of an "insider" strategy included funding demonstration projects to provide strong examples of successful educational experiments, or as the interviewee described:

> *The kind of "yes we can" examples to help people see that ordinary educators in ordinary school systems can actually make things happen that are quite different. We do not believe in the "superman" theory. We believe in trying to show that ordinary people in communities can make this happen.*

"Insider" work incorporated demonstration projects similar to Broad's work on pay-for-performance in Washington, DC. Ford has funded experiments in urban centers related to budgeting, as one staff member explained:

> *In Los Angeles, we're funding some of the pilot schools and the zone of choice schools where they're really trying to change how budgeting gets done, where the union has agreed to a thin contract so that some of those system changes will be examples of how that could move.*

Insider strategies also included building systems capacity with government institutions, as one respondent related:

> *We've been working with the US Department of Education, thinking about how to use the flexibility that comes with the ESEA [Elementary and Secondary Education Act] waivers that states are applying for to really push this more and better learning time in those neighborhoods of concentrated poverty and racial isolation—how to make it possible to use this flexibility in the waiver to really build a capacity of systems to do this kind of work.*

Unions represented another significant "insider" ally that Ford sought to partner with:

> *We do grant making to the unions for some union-led initiatives, knowing that in order for dramatic change to be possible and sustained, the teachers' unions have to see it as part of their own agenda for schools, and that they're really involved in helping to shape it, and then you can use the collective bargaining agreement as a way to build system capacity to make something happen.*

In a notable development, several interviewees commented that Ford's culture had begun to change under Luis Ubiñas, president of the Ford Foundation from 2009–2013 and a former director of McKinsey & Co., a global strategy consulting firm. During this time, informants explained, Ford's strategies had moved toward a greater emphasis on a foundation-centric locus of control and more emphasis on elite engagement, in contrast with the foundation's historical value on relinquishing tighter control at the foundation level. One former Ford staff member noted that the foundation's approach toward grantee management had "totally changed" in comparison to earlier decades:

> Now at Ford, there's a much more particular narrow gauge program piece. [It's] "We're going to support certain kinds of principals and teachers in certain selected cities because our theory is that we need to demonstrate that this particular kind of school reform effort is successful and we're going to go find people who agree with it and give them money." There is much more staff intervention with a grantee. Now they're more stratified bureaucracies. [They say, "If] you agree with us, we'll give you the money, and we'd actually like to run the project by the way"—much like Gates.

Another official noted that internal changes in staffing at Ford, with more officials entering the foundation from managerial backgrounds, had introduced more contention around some key assumptions of the foundation's grant-making culture. For example, Ford's proclivity to invest in long-term capacity-building initiatives with core operating support, as opposed to shorter-term projects, was challenged by staff members who believed that initiatives should be designed to target more concrete projects with defined timelines and outcomes. One informant explained this dynamic:

> Increasingly at Ford, there's that internal tension because there are different kinds of people within Ford. These are some major changes, and they are happening because you're bringing adults with different kind[s] of training and different kind[s] of tools to bear.

Other Ford respondents, however, noted that most staff members were able to negotiate the tension between strategic management and value-oriented community engagement. One described the situation as follows:

People who come here have a set of values, so I think it's easier for us to try to strike a balance between being strategic and staying really grounded in this value of engagement and democratic participation in the work. It's just the people who want to work here believe that.

The Puzzle of Balancing Grasstops and Grassroots

What, then, is the best way to design a strategy for desired social change—to incorporate the expertise of elites as a first-order priority or to incorporate community engagement from the outset? At the core of foundations' differing approaches lie tensions about the value of democratically generated input, which interviewees sometimes viewed as a hindrance to efficiency and effectiveness. While acknowledging the need for broad-based support of policy reforms, foundation officials showed internal reticence about being "held back" by the glacial pace of local community politics, in addition to lack of policy-related expertise on the part of community members. This reticence was particularly evident at Gates and also, to a lesser extent, at Broad, both of which held "urgency" and fast timelines as core values in their grant making—values that respondents feared were not necessarily well served by democratic processes. One Gates official commented on this concern:

How do you establish a bottom-up versus top-down mix? It's a puzzle we've never resolved. It is very tricky—at the beginning we were too top-down, but bottom-up seldom came up with breakthrough thinking, the higher risk, what was possible without constraints [types of ideas]. The "big think" things came from a tight group of people with a blank sheet of paper.

Foundations' balancing of the tensions between "big think" versus "bottom-up," as this source described, represents a fundamental distinction that extends beyond their selection of grantees and partners, and into the core of their management of day-to-day work—how they approach problems, frame solutions, and evaluate their results, which I explore in the next chapter.

5

"We Wish There Was an App for That"

Framing Problems and Evaluating Results

The four foundations evidenced distinct differences regarding how they framed and approached social problems, and how they managed solutions—including the results they expected and the types of expertise that they engaged. Gates and Broad tended to frame problems in a "technical" fashion, preferring to address social issues that have a clear solution and where a causal link exists between the problem and the results, consistent with the norms of engineering as a discipline.[1] By contrast, Kellogg and Ford primarily framed problems in an "adaptive" way, viewing problems as caused by multifaceted factors that are frequently political, social, and cultural in nature and cannot be solved through technical intervention. (See Figure 5.1.)

One significant distinction between technical and adaptive problems is that technical problems are amenable to having "large amounts of money injected into them in the short term" in order to achieve

FIGURE 5.1   Framing problems: Technical versus adaptive

Outcome-oriented approach	Technical	Adaptive	Field-oriented approach
	• Foundations pursue initiatives that have a causal link between a problem and a solution and may be solved by technical interventions	• Foundations pursue initiatives that are more complex, multifaceted, and caused by multiple factors	

impact, according to one interviewee, who gave the example of providing vaccines on a massive scale to eradicate communicable diseases in the developing world. However, most social problems can be framed either as technical or adaptive at some level. In the example of the microfinance field, large cash infusions would have an impact on poverty, in the short term, but might not address institutional problems related to gender dynamics or health issues in impoverished communities. One Ford source illustrated the distinction between approaches as the difference between a "technical-scientific approach" and a "behavioral-humanistic approach" to illustrate a contrast between Ford and other foundations:

> In the AIDS arena, [other foundations] are heavily involved in the vaccine development, the scientific side of it. Ford is heavily involved in the humanistic side of it because part of the problem is cultural. Some people don't want to take their medications because of the stigma behind it. Some people won't want to use condoms or those kinds of things because of their own beliefs about it. And so, therefore, you need to have a community education strategy that soften[s] the human side of the problem.

Likewise, another Ford respondent also referred to Gates as "much more technical and scientifically oriented," and to Ford as subscribing to "the humanistic side."

TECHNICAL PROBLEMS

Gates, particularly in its early years, explicitly preferred not to make grants to the "humanistic side," instead focusing on approaches that reflected its benefactors' engineering roots. Jokingly, one Gates official mentioned that "we wish there was an app" for solutions that required engagement with more complicated political and social issues. Bill Gates himself told a *New York Times* reporter, "We're technocrats."[2]

As an example, several informants referred to Gates's and Broad's interest in expanding the number of high-quality charter schools through funding charter school management organizations as a technical approach, or what some described as a "silver bullet." One interviewee described:

> *That is a very big ethos within mainstream philanthropy and could be very appealing now in terms of advocacy and policy involvement, to say, "We want to focus on the problem. Okay, you say, charter schools are the answer."*

Another respondent, a professor, made a similar observation, saying that Gates, Broad, and other foundations with similar approaches embraced "the standard reform package of choice, outcomes, alternative pathways and charters," which represented an "overly simplistic" approach. This source argued (facetiously):

> *Charters are a vehicle for experimentation, but [don't] necessarily do it all. Without dealing with instruction in the end, the actual practice, rather than just the outcomes (and killing half the teachers), that whole business is too crude a model.*

Several respondents pointed to Gates's and Broad's tendency to specify desired results of programs in advance, which many viewed as a challenge in terms of adapting to midcourse corrections. A Gates official commented on this dynamic:

> *That's one of the downsides of being a tightly focused strategic organization, and sometimes if you don't leave room for innovation, you might not look to that next frontier if it doesn't fit in your strategy at the current time.*

Another Gates grantee related a similar story, stating, "They want you to tell them your results before you even get the money." One interviewee, a former foundation president, told a similar story regarding Gates's desired entry into digital learning:

> Gates was interested in getting into the digital space, and [the digital learning expert] started laughing at [the Gates program officer]. He said, "What's so funny? Why are you laughing at me?" And [the digital learning expert] said, "When you make a grant in digital learning, you just can't predict what you're going to find out. It's exploratory. People can't tell you in advance exactly what their timetable is going to be and exactly what kind of outcomes they're going to have. You guys can't do that. It's impossible for you to do that. You just should stay the hell away from this because it's just not anything you're wired up to do." And [the Gates program officer] said, "It's really true. We just are not built that way. We have a driven couple at the head of this family foundation and they want results yesterday or the day before, and we're going to pursue strategies to the nth degree that we already decided, so it's a very different relationship."

One interviewee, a professor, reflected on how Gates and Broad might have reacted to the New Standards Project, an initiative that did not achieve its predetermined goals but was ultimately considered a landmark effort in the field in other ways:

> If you'd had to make a judgment about, bottom-line, was the New Standards Project a success or a failure? If you made the judgment based on what the New Standards folk proposed to do and how they proposed to be held accountable, you would have said "failure," because their goal was to build a national examination system that [...] a quarter of the nation's kids would be participating in—a much more sophisticated system that holds portfolios and projects. And at the end of the grant period, [only] two small states had adopted the New Standards exams, as well as some scattering

of districts in New York. But if you took the longer view about the impact of that project—the people that it attracted, recruited, trained, developed the image of what a high-quality aligned standards and assessment would look like—it [advanced the conversation] in a whole different way that you couldn't have predicted. My fear is that places like Gates and Broad might have shut that project down.

Adaptive Problems

Gates and Broad preferred to fund initiatives that targeted defined, delineated outcomes, rather than funding the overall infrastructure and management capacity of organizations or institutions. In contrast, both Kellogg and Ford emphasized multifaceted approaches and building the capacity of institutions, which they often referred to as "field-building," as opposed to targeted, project-specific initiatives. One Ford official deadpanned, "There's no vaccine for public education," arguing, "It's about building a field as opposed to injecting a specific idea or a specific technical solution. And it's what some people might say old school—that's just not how the Gates and the Broads do it anymore." A Kellogg official made a similar statement, emphasizing the long-term nature of the foundation's policy work: "[With] good policy influencing you have to be in there for the long haul and just kind of stick, stick, stick."

One informant explained these distinct philosophies as a major dividing line within the field of philanthropy: "There is such a range from 'Here's some general support, we believe in your organization,' to 'Here's a project grant and we want exactly these kind of outcomes.'" A Kellogg staff member described this tension in the following way:

Foundations are not always interested in funding the process. They want to fund the outcomes. They want to fund the program. But I think from a civic engagement standpoint, we have very few NGOs who exist to help the community do an ongoing community solutions process that's seen as infrastructure overhead or process, not outcomes. It's a very worthwhile investment for a foundation, [but most foundations would not say] "Fund the process; fund the backbone."

Another Ford respondent described this dynamic as a "huge continuing problem in the field," arguing "There haven't been enough foundations willing to invest in building intermediate institutions. There's still this bias toward projects rather than institution building or field building." One interviewee, a philanthropic consultant, commented on the dominance of a "problem-solving approach" and its rise in the past decade, particularly surrounding the emergence of Gates and Broad as philanthropic leaders:

More foundations are engaging in advocacy now than ten years ago or even five years ago, and I think that's going to increase even more because there are more foundations that are taking a problem-solving approach to issues. Any foundation that's engaged in that kind of problem-solving inquiry is going to very quickly realize that policy advocacy is likely to be part of the solution. That sort of problem-solving mentality is something I see picking up more and more.

At Kellogg and Ford, staff members pushed back against these changing norms and the perceived prevalence of a "problem-solving mentality" in the philanthropic profession. Instead, they described their desired outcomes using terms such as "changing the conversation," "advancing learning," "elevating awareness," and other intangible factors as opposed to specific "wins." At Kellogg in particular, staff eschewed the suggestion that legislative outcomes were an ultimate goal. One official described the foundation's work in early childhood education in the following way:

We might be very strong supporters of Dream Act–type legislation because of what it does for vulnerable kids and families, but it wouldn't be a single issue for us. For us, even if you passed it, [we'd ask] "What do we know about English language learners and how they acquire language, or how [you do] it with dual language families? So we might be very interested in supporting Dream Act–like legislation, but it would be part of a larger portfolio."

Another Kellogg staffer agreed, stating: "Rather than just say, 'Okay, the victory was the policy,' [we need] just a more complete picture of all the things that need to work to effectuate the outcome you're looking for." One Kellogg informant explained this perspective as a "multi-pronged" approach rather than a "silver bullet":

Everybody [in the field of philanthropy] is looking for that silver bullet. I think we try to get away from it in the sense that we do a multipronged investment. We think through how it's going to interact with other stuff. It's not just about passing teacher tenure laws.

These statements contrast starkly with statements from Gates and Broad respondents, who emphasized the end goal of major policy changes as driving forces in their strategies and theories of change. For example, one Gates interviewee shared that "our outcomes were to get public policies changed," and a Broad official stated:

We recently changed our strategic defining process and so for the next three years [2011–2014], really our number one priority is policy, and we say that we're going to be successful when we see a strong reauthorization of the Elementary and Secondary [Education] Act.

EVALUATING RESULTS: QUANTIFIABLE VERSUS INTEGRATED

Foundations' differential framing of problems also dovetailed with the types of methodologies and metrics they used to measure their success (see Figure 5.2). Generally, Gates and Broad tended to seek results that were attributable to the foundation's funding and numerically measurable in nature. Kellogg and Ford evidenced what informants described

FIGURE 5.2   Evaluating results: Quantifiable versus integrated

Outcome-oriented approach	Quantifiable	Integrated	Field-oriented approach
	• Foundations prefer to evaluate initiatives using quantitative data to establish proof of impact	• Foundations value both qualitative and quantitative data in their assessment of programs	

as a "holistic" or "integrated" approach, wherein they were more comfortable with a variety of intangible indicators and less concrete results in addition to quantitative metrics.[3]

Quantifiable Results

Gates and Broad, particularly earlier in their histories, generally expected proof of impact, especially in Broad's case. Broad was notable for its emphasis on achieving "early results" with "dramatic effects," as one interviewee described, highlighting one investment that the foundation was particularly pleased with:

I would have been disappointed had we not seen a significant—i.e., at least a 5 percent—improvement in student achievement. Some of the schools did dramatically better than that. They literally doubled their math scores. It was immediate and dramatic.

Several Broad staff members indicated that their grantees were expected to achieve outcomes within a short amount of time, enabling Broad to assess the returns on its grant making. One source described:

Eli Broad is distinctive because his conception of accountability is [such that] to give money to a school, [the foundation] needs to see the test scores rise after one year.

A former Gates official similarly remarked on Gates's and Broad's desire to establish attributable results and establish causality in interventions on short timelines: "I think there's this desire to see not only early results, but results that you can quantify in a discrete way as having come from your foundation."

A Broad official described how accountability worked at the foundation through performance metrics, which were determined at the outset of a grantee relationship through contract terms:

If your [charter] school is not performing well, you don't have a permanent right to operate—you're held accountable. There's a mechanism for transparency and bringing in someone else who can do better. We do that by setting up a clear set of performance metrics upfront, which are negotiated. We agree that if you don't [meet the goals], if you underperform, [the relationship] doesn't go on for forty years. We're very serious about holding folks accountable and giving those [who are achieving their goals] more opportunities to do more, like opening another school.

During the past several years, however, as Gates and Broad have become more deeply invested in policy-related initiatives, both foundations have made shifts in the types of interventions and initiatives that they chose to fund, as well as their expectations of grantees. According to one Broad staff member, "Rather than doing direct funding, the foundation is now looking at the policies that would create an infrastructure under the national level to support those [interventions] happening." Similarly, one Gates source described how the foundation was slowly incorporating strategies that were more characteristic of adaptive framing, describing it as a "major change of heart":

There was a huge change in how [the foundation] was acting, and they had gone from targeted grants around specific areas to a period of time when they were really investing in wholesale district reform. So some people were going in and saying, "Well, we're here to work on teacher quality, but as we work on teacher quality, gee whiz, what we're seeing is that one of the great impediments to effective teaching is the central office. So we've got to work on a much more holistic set of reform issues if we're going to get to where we want to go."

A Gates official described how this change occurred:

We got more sophisticated about the education space, and we began to see that no matter how many charter schools, you're still talking about a small fraction of kids. I think even your biggest charter supporters would say that that promise [of charter schools] hasn't been realized, and as a result, if you want to try to dramatically improve outcomes for all students, then you're going to have to look at the system changes.

Multiple informants noted that Gates has recently reconsidered some of its views toward measurement. This change in thinking underscores how Gates's increasing emphasis on policy had necessitated an acknowledgment that policy efforts would entail an institutional tolerance for longer-term timelines and reconceptualizing their expectations for quantification and measurement. This change was also due, in part, to lessons learned from investments that were unsuccessful. Several Gates officials described the difficulty the foundation had faced distilling cultural and social factors into causal models. As one former staff member described:

One of the things that would drive me up the wall—they put arrows between boxes and they think that it means a causal relationship. I don't know that I find a lot of foundations that are doing strategic philanthropy that able to chart a logic model.

This challenge sometimes resulted in projects that were ended prematurely, due to failure to achieve planned impact. One Gates interviewee described how initial negative results from evaluations of the small schools initiative's first years led to early termination of a major evaluation contract and subsequently of the small schools work itself:

The evaluations were very critical, [showing] that in some grade levels, small schools had no impact on achievement. Because [the foundation's leadership] didn't like what they were seeing in the evaluations, they decided to end the contract.

Multiple interviewees noted that the failure of the small schools initiative had led to Gates reconsidering some of its views toward measurement and tight adherence toward prespecified goals. One respondent commented:

I give Gates high marks for [acknowledging that] while there were some things that clearly worked, there was a lot that didn't work and that we learned from, and we are in the learning business. We're moving in a different direction, but it's not as if we're saying that was a failure.

Other respondents noted that Gates was laudable for its transparency about its failures and adjusting its strategy based on new information. One stated:

You get the sense they've been really smart, thoughtful, deliberate in building staff capacity, learning as they go, investing in data. They [no longer] have an overly simplistic view of what it's going to take. One of the questions is how much you're able to learn and grow and deepen in your understanding of the work, and they've been really good about that. I think they really came to appreciate just how complicated and complex making change is in the public sector.

A former Gates staffer also reflected on Gates's evolution over its relatively brief fifteen-year history, stating that the culture of Gates had changed to address critiques about its perceived "arrogance" in the field of education, which the official felt reflected an "engineering mentality" focused on problem solving as opposed to understanding a given context. The informant explained:

[In the beginning] they had good impulses to efficiency, but didn't quite get to empathy. [Now] they're rooting their language about solutions in the language of those who came before, with more respect. They're developing better relationships with the people

they work with. It was clunky at first, but it's more well oiled now, and they're being thoughtful about their relationships.

Likewise, Broad's redirection of a larger proportion of its resources on policy influence also catalyzed internal reflection and changes. One Broad staff member explained this shift over the past several years and how it had changed the structure of the foundation's measurement approaches:

Because of the complexity around changing policy, while we say we can promote mayoral control, it's very unique to each individual case that we look at, and it's also very hard to talk about whether or not we've been effective in the methods that we used to implement that strategy. So while it's easy to say, "The big win would be if Mayor Antonio Villaraigosa is able to take over LAUSD," I think in the longer run, it's whether or not we were able to really help support [that goal], and I think we still do this with almost all our grantees. So we might not be able to carry out the end goal, but we can definitely provide money to help them get to a certain place where they can make an informed decision. We can also provide them with either knowledge or networks or connections that we have. And so even though the end result might not be [that] they got mayoral control, I think we can still sometimes see value in the work that we've done, and think that we handled it as successfully as possible given the legal constraints.

Another Broad informant explained their changing approach in a similar way, reflecting a longer-term view of policy change:

It's sort of in some ways like a staircase, right? [Some of our past work's results] weren't as radical as you would have liked them to have been, but it was a good start, and then the policy environment becomes more welcoming to that, which means the next set of efforts can be hopefully more radical and dramatic in terms of their impact and reach and effectiveness. So, for example, we did some good work with Education Trust West around highlighting the issue of teacher salary and equity, and the assignment of teachers and the interplay with Title 1 and the comparability provisions were essentially leading to a situation where poor kids weren't getting Title 1 as an add-on; they were getting it as a backfill. That was something that we've highlighted that turns out is something that Chairman Miller believes is important, and it's likely some change will be included in the Elementary and Secondary Education Act Reauthorization.

Like Gates, Broad staff members also expressed a desire to become more effective with their grantees in terms of building relationships. One described:

[Many of] our grantees have been in business for a long time, and we're doing a lot of constituency building, understanding what their assets are and that they can bring important things. We're trying to figure out how to do our work more effectively with deeper engagement [in communities]—we've gotten better in the last three to five years.

Reflecting these developments, Broad respondents pointed to efforts to "change the conversation" as an important element of the foundation's new strategic plan—language more frequently associated with Kellogg and Ford. Respondents' descriptions of newer evaluation processes and methods at both Gates and Broad showed more tolerance for less quantifiable outcomes and more assessments that established plausible and defensible contributions rather than causal attribution. One Broad official remarked:

Some policy work either you didn't measure it per se, but it clearly had an impact beyond what you could say. When your agenda is pretty similar to what the administration is doing, you've been able to have some impact. Was it all us? No, but you can say, yeah, there was some impact here.

As an example, the informant described Broad's work on the "Ed in '08" campaign with Gates, a $60 million joint-funding effort that aimed to position education as a priority platform agenda item in the presidential campaign through targeted marketing and advocacy campaigns. The Ed in '08 campaign was broadly viewed as unsuccessful, which this official reflected on:

> *Our work was [in] two pieces. One was "Can we wake up the American public and try and ensure that education is a key issue?" We did not have much success in that area. [Two], "Can we put a set of policy recommendations on the table that will be attractive to presidential candidates and to the policy world and would have impact going forward?" On that one, I think we get a home run. So some things even within the same project work well and other things don't.*

Integrated Results

Along these lines, Kellogg and Ford sources were explicit in their critique of causal attribution of results, instead seeking plausible and defensible evidence of impact as opposed to proof. One Ford official remarked, "The movement in philanthropy towards attribution of impact, that's to say a straight line from a foundation to policy outcome, is problematic." Another Ford staff member noted, "There's no foundation theory of change that you can trace back and say, 'As a result of their action, these policies are X.'" Similarly, one Kellogg respondent argued, "It isn't just about the *wins* you get. Given all the complex dynamics of politics and Congress, you can't control the different variables." Another Kellogg official commented:

> *Support[ing] the interests of people in communities, supporting institutions, supporting individuals who have a particular perspective or validation of leaders in the community allows you to say, "We supported these people, [but] we can't attribute." We can't take credit for any of the stuff they actually do other than to say*

that we supported their work more generally. What you want to say at the end of the day is that that investment caused people to stand up and take note and make a change.

A Ford official echoed this sentiment, questioning methods of quantitative evaluation that isolated the impact of a single foundation and were driven by a theory of change:

We're thinking about [our work] as a collective evaluation process—about what our contribution is within an ecosystem of players. We've become much more modest about outcomes and more humble about what we can do. We're rejecting these purely scientific, rational grant-making viewpoints. [Foundation] metrics are usually like, "A leads to B and then this will eventually happen." Foundation[s] can sit in an ivory tower and predict, "Here's how the world's going to work over the next twenty years." We just don't think that's reasonable anymore.

One Ford respondent noted that many foundations, adhering to the managerial principles of strategic philanthropy, were often reluctant to "fund things which explicitly did not make a return on investment [and] could not be measured using short-term metrics." This respondent, who had also worked extensively with Gates, provided a specific example of how Gates staff members began to move away from a decision-making process that emphasized return on investment:

The Gates Foundation had started out by saying, "Why don't we focus on the hardest-to-serve populations?" And they were thinking, "Let's do some strategy around men and boys of color." And they wound up not doing that at all because their analysis using traditional [leading strategy consulting firm] McKinsey [tools] was small populations, high cost, not a very good use for your dollar. A better use of the dollar was to try to find something that for a smaller cost would cover a bigger population. And that's where they ultimately went with their education program. It was partly because of the questions the strategists were asking and the tools that they were using brought the foundation's focus away from the hardest-to-serve populations.

Another Ford official mentioned that the capacity for quantitatively measuring outcomes had changed within the broader field of philanthropy and that nonrigorous evaluation techniques were no longer considered acceptable:

What changed is in part the capacity of the social and behavioral science research community, the applied research communities, to pilot large amounts of data and to define what should be done by what they are capable of measuring by saying, "You could do this, but it can't be measured. Therefore, it's not worth doing."

Kellogg respondents spoke to this challenge, noting that emphasis on measurement had resulted in significant discussion about how to measure complex constructs such as "racial healing" and other major facets of their work. For example, one Kellogg official noted, "We are developing scorecards and assessments that measure public voice, racial equity, social justice and community systems, social determinants of health problems. It's not neat and clean." One Ford staff member described the foundation's "struggle" with choosing appropriate indicators as evidence of success, explaining how Ford deliberately approached measurement of results:

The emphasis here is we will never let our work be reduced to only things that can be counted. We are paying very much attention to our impact but not in a simplistic easily countable way. We have to think very strategically about indicators that don't become the thing in itself. So we wouldn't want to just count the number of schools that have expanded learning time because that in itself would not accomplish these larger purposes that we have in mind. [We track] the extent to which the conversation starts turning in this direction, things like the elected officials who take this on, the extent to which you see it in newspapers, people start talking about it.

One Ford interviewee described the process by which it arrived at the indicators it planned to use for its new inequality work, which reflected adaptive framing that focused on cultural norms:

Our first step is to get our grantees to think through, in partnership with experts, what has driven inequality? We have identified some drivers of inequality by putting all our grantees together and asking them what we saw as drivers of inequality across the world, like discrimination, market ideology, a poor social contract, dominant cultural narratives. The kinds of things we're toying with as indicators of success include to what extent do we help the government support advocates to best organize people so they can participate; to what extent do we help ensure community benefits in any development project accrue to a neighborhood in order to ensure some level of jobs.

Another interviewee discussed recent attempts at Gates to expand its thinking about its emphasis on outcomes in its strategic decision-making processes, rather than relying strictly on a strict cost-benefit framework:

Now many of these foundations [. . .], having won on the policy side, are going back and they are trying to find places to build the capacity, to demonstrate [. . .] and blah, blah, blah. But that wasn't the way they started. That was not their strategy. Their strategy was at the top. And that's very different. It also changes the way that the foundation does business in a very fundamental way. And their own ambivalence . . . they look back and they think they made a mistake. They think that they forgot to put the values back into their analysis. Economists are not trained to do that.

"Putting the values back" into strategic grant making, as this respondent notes, implies a significant shift in how foundations that predominantly align with an outcome-oriented approach view their core operations—and, interestingly, recalls some Kellogg informants' views about the difficulties of achieving strategic goals in a highly value-driven environment. Thus, foundations face tensions between engaging with problems in highly technical ways that tend to exclude "messier" approaches to framing issues and measuring results versus operating in an adaptive fashion that may address the complexity of deeply rooted and multifaceted social problems but lack the capacity to produce accelerated impact, preferring instead to "stick, stick, stick," in the words of one source, over the course of decades. Both paths contain unique challenges and implications, particularly in the field of education—which, due to the involvement of outcome-oriented foundations, has seen more change in the last fifteen years than it has in the past century.

6

"It's Singularly Because of Gates and Broad"

Critiques and Implications of Foundation Activism

During the past ten years, foundation involvement in policy has become highly visible, particularly at the federal level, and to a degree not seen since the 1960s and the Ford Foundation's Gray Areas effort. Through support of competitive federal grant programs, foundations have contributed not only funding but also expertise and political influence to directly shape new policy directions at the US Department of Education, including two competitive funding opportunities, Race to the Top and the Investing in Innovation (i3) Fund.[1] To compete for the Race to the Top program's $4 billion in funds, states were required to institutionalize a series of reforms similar to many foundations' espoused priorities, such as lifting caps on charter schools and establishing state standards that aligned with the Common Core State Standards. Similarly, the i3 fund was capitalized by a group of twelve private foundations, which granted $500 million to "leverage" the US Department of Education's $650 million fund to scale effective models of improving student achievement. According to the Department of Education, the grant was targeted to support the department's "similarly aligned investments." Vartan Gregorian, president of the Carnegie Corporation of New York, stated, "Much of what Secretary [Arne] Duncan is currently addressing at the Department builds on existing foundation investments in education."[2]

This close coupling of foundations with government is the result of a deliberate strategy by outcome-oriented foundations to pursue a coordinated suite of education reforms in partnership with government in order to produce the most concentrated impact. This "convergence" strategy, as Reckhow termed it, involves an elite cohort of foundations, education nonprofits, corporate leaders engaged in education, and urban superintendents who are "impatient with public bureaucracies."[3, 4] By engaging a small group of elites and experts, and working in partnership with like-minded leaders, these foundations attempt to avoid the often dysfunctional political dynamics of government bureaucracies to advance desired policy targets more quickly and efficiently. One Ford interviewee commented on the degree to which Gates's and Broad's efforts had resulted in changing federal policy strategies:

> It was not that long ago, if anyone had come to us and said, "In the next few years someone is going to come along and within eighteen to twenty-four months, they are going to convince the right people with a certain amount of grants to embrace a national core curriculum," which is something that has invaded and people just thought that was like the third rail. You can't touch that in American politics. But we now have a Common Core, and we are slowly moving to a common protocol for teacher evaluations.

Another respondent, a former Gates official, agreed, stating, "I am amazed at what they've done. Look at how education is a high-priority item in this country. And it's singularly because of Gates and Broad."

Although this strategy has been largely successful in advancing policy goals, it has also sparked the majority of critiques of foundations, especially Gates and Broad, in the last several years. In fact, a critique reminiscent of objections in the 1969 Tax Reform Act hearings arose in the media in 2011, questioning the extent to which foundations and the state reflect common objectives as well as common alumni. deMarrais summarized the substance of these concerns:

Activity in support of new federal policies reflects a shared vision and a deliberate determination by policymakers to engage funders. Many of the policies currently promoted by the Department of Education have been supported and advanced by funders . . . there has been a high degree of communication with and collaboration between the philanthropic and public sectors, especially at the federal level . . . this has been driven by an alignment of ideas and strategies and abetted by personal connections between the two sectors.[5]

Echoing this argument, Thomas Payzant, the former superintendent of Boston public schools, noted: "The focus of the [policy] work has been narrowed to what the foundations believe will give the most leverage for change and improvement."[6] Vicki Phillips, elementary and secondary education director at the Gates Foundation, echoed Payzant: "There's definitely a convergence of ideas, not just between us and the administration but between us and many other reform-minded people who have been working on these issues for a long time."[7] One interviewee expressed a concern with foundation-endorsed reforms being adopted as federal policy:

I think there is a feeling that it's the Gates Foundation agenda that the administration has employed on the education side, and I don't think that's good for them. I think [it] has the appearance that they're bringing in all these people to advocate a specific set of goals that are tied to what the Gates Foundation thinks is best.

[Secretary] Arne [Duncan] made a conscious decision that Gates's world was the way.

One respondent, a historian, compared Gates's largess in federal education policy to Ford's efforts in the 1960s, remarking on their qualitative differences:

We have a very successful attempt to set public policy—not just influencing, but purchasing public policy. If you compare this to the reaction against the Ford Foundation around 1969, what's interesting is that Gates is strong-arming public policy in a way the Ford Foundation never would have thought of doing . . . there is a certain asymmetry in how the folks who are trying to promote reforms today are being discussed contrary to how, say, the Ford Foundation or Annenberg were. The Gates people make [former Ford Foundation president] Mac Bundy look like a midget.

Some Gates respondents themselves expressed discomfort with the extent to which the foundation had partnered with the Department of Education. One Gates official commented on the appearance of collusion between Gates and the federal government:

There was this kind of twinkle in the eye of one of our [leaders] when the Obama administration's education policy framework [emerged], and this person said, "Aren't we lucky that the Obama administration's education agenda is so compatible with ours?" And then there came the twinkle, right? You know, we wouldn't take credit out loud even amongst ourselves. But, you know, the twinkle.

The interviewee elaborated on the "uncomfortable" normative implications that this convergence suggested but also noted that these issues typically did not receive attention:

For organizations with our size and with our resources, you can make grants to lots of organizations to promote a certain message not just with government but also with business and with the public, and anybody who cares to look would find very quickly that all of these organizations suddenly singing from the same hymn book are all getting money from the same organization. We fund almost everyone who does advocacy. We have this enormous power to sway the public conversations about things like effective teaching or standards and mobilizing lots of resources in their favor without real robust debate. I mean, it's striking to me actually.

Interviewees described concerns about the potential for large foundations to concentrate resources toward common goals. As one respondent described: "Foundations joining together collectively to build momentum: I think that's dangerous for society and for the foundation world. It gives weapons to people who basically don't like the idea of foundations." Similarly, one interviewee noted, "I think the very concept of a multitude of voices and independent views and differences of opinions and not being monolithic [are] all threatened to some extent by too much concentration." Another respondent concurred, highlighting the "worst-case scenario" of convergence between foundations that are also closely coupled with government:

The worst case for my mind is the one that we're actually in, where you have one particularly large foundation, a fair degree of coherence among several like-minded foundations, and a pretty close working relationship with the federal government. At that point, rather than being sources of competing ideas and sources of alternate ways of doing, foundations working in concert with government start to feel a lot like there's a real risk that you wind up supporting group think.

Interviewees also expressed concerns that the tightly coupled relationships between foundations and government, which drove the implementation of reforms, might become unsustainable when political administrations changed. While elite, expert-driven agendas might enable a more streamlined policy process, the resulting reforms could fall short of their intended impact in the absence of leadership sympathetic to foundations' priorities. One respondent described how a philanthropic initiative that was dependent on close relationships between individuals in foundations and government was hindered when faced with a leadership change:

As [Gates and Broad] became more involved in district reform, they began to look at pressure points or leverage points with school systems and essentially attempted to work or establish and maintain very close relationships with school superintendents. The foundations saw themselves, particularly the front-line program officers and their bosses saw themselves, as intimately and intricately engaged in helping to formulate new reform strategies within a district, and would consider themselves close allies of the superintendent. So superintendents would come and go, and the relationships between funders and superintendents would change. And there was almost a trajectory that would follow from great hope to this wonderful knight who was going to save everything. Now, what they did not do very well is engage boards of education.

As a result, the respondent shared, foundations began to learn that boards of education were important constituents that also possessed power, and some foundations began to work more closely with them, in some cases securing agreements with board members to continue reforms even after superintendents depart. However, informants also noted that foundations' interest in maintaining relationships with district leaders was sometimes undermined by their tendency to change course in their strategies. Respondents expressed concerns that foundations' pursuit of mid-course corrections had a tendency to damage not only foundations' credibility within the education field, but also their effectiveness. As one source from Gates related:

If the foundation changes its mind from the point of view of just someone looking at the outside, and all of the sudden [funding] dries up pretty quickly and nobody returns your phone calls anymore, right? It's a hard way not just to make a living but also to drive effective social change from the grassroots.

This challenges a core assumption about the value that foundations add to policy contexts through experimentation and innovation outside the constraint of state bureaucracy. Foundations' experimentation, especially in the field of education reform, often takes place in low-income communities, where repercussions can be significant if foundations exit. Several sources characterized the end of Gates's small schools initiative as an example, wherein grantees experienced widespread confusion and anxiety. In earlier research, I interviewed a Gates official who related, "All of a sudden, small schools are it—the panacea. Then [we] change [our mind] . . . we behave as if nothing's changed, whereas almost all our grantees from the decade are like 'what happened to you guys?'"[8]

Along these lines, informants referred to the metaphor of a chessboard to explain their relationships with some foundation staff members. One stated, "When you do have a relationship with foundations [with a less managerial approach], they tend to be pretty hands off. Whereas sometimes you get the feeling with the new foundations that they see you like a pawn on their chessboard." Another source used nearly identical phrasing, noting, "You always feel like a piece on the chessboard." One Gates staff member acknowledged this dynamic, describing it as pervasive:

I think the foundation–grantee relationship is fraught with peril around the balance of power and lack of humility on the part of program officers, and the micromanaging the program officers can do, and looking to impose their strategies and their ideas upon grantees, and grantees not feeling enabled or empowered or comfortable enough to stand up to any of those situations.

Along these lines, many informants described how "well-meaning" elites from "the new foundations," emboldened by success in the private sector, sought to impose solutions within the field of education, often in organizations where these actions were not necessarily contextually appropriate. One respondent explained this dynamic:

> *Where we've got into trouble with that is where I think you have elites who [are] well meaning because they run their organization successfully, and [have] made a lot of money. They look at the social sector and make that same judgment about what's wrong with the social sector. And in a lot of cases, those assumptions aren't right [and] their process for changing it is to use their same power and savvy networks within the elite to make things happen.*

A Gates source noted that a "growing concern [exists] about whether education reform is driven too much by wealthy people who don't really understand." Another stated: "People see [foundations] as outsiders coming in because they have a lot of money and trying to dictate to states and school districts what the best thing is. I think some of these districts . . . the opponents think you don't know our community, so you come in here with a lot of money and tell us what to do." One former Gates official commented on the distinctions between philanthropists, elite intellectuals, and the communities they targeted:

> *Sometimes I thought the foundation spent too much time on what it believed was the right way. I often thought there was a little bit of a disconnect between what, generally speaking, highly educated white academics believe is the right way and the reality of what happens. You can't just go in and start criticizing [school districts populated predominantly by minorities] if you really don't understand everything that's going on.*

A Ford source made a similar comment:

> *Now I think people feel they know the answer and even if that means curtailing public debates or favoring one group over another systemically and aggressively, that's okay, and that for me crosses the line because [the only answer] that's going to sustain itself by*

gaining broad popular support in the long term is by [working with communities].

In some cases, informants reported that foundations that aligned with an outcome-oriented approach sometimes held negative attitudes toward community members and school district employees. One informant noted, "Now, [education philanthropy] suffers from an underlying feeling that people aren't trying . . . [foundation officers think] 'The real problem is stupidity!'" Several interviewees from nonprofit organizations in the education sector noted that they had experienced foundation staff who had described teachers, nonprofit leaders, or administrators as lazy and ill equipped with the appropriate expertise that would enable them to "just solve the problem," as one source stated.

Interviewees also raised questions about the extent to which the "new foundations" understood educational contexts and practice. One Ford respondent described her resistance to norms in education philanthropy regarding business expertise:

Essentially if you get really smart people who understand good business strategies, it doesn't so much matter if they're grounded in communities or if they're grounded in depth in the areas of [education policy] that they're working in. The same kind of people go to McKinsey or Bain or the Boston Consulting Group. It's very attractive in philanthropy, but I think that it makes philanthropy much more removed from the problems in this authentic and democratic way.

One interviewee, a professor, noted that the managerial expertise that characterized Gates and Broad exemplified an increasingly prevalent "consultant mentality" within the field of philanthropy, explaining that many high-level officials at these foundations had come to the foundations from "strategic planning land [and] consulting shops." Several other respondents commented that management consultants from high-profile firms such as Bridgespan, Bain, Parthenon, and McKinsey had assumed central roles in foundation decision making about strategy at Gates and Broad, while a former Ford official joked, "Armadas of consultants float around on Gates money." One Gates official noted, somewhat sarcastically, that some decisions in the education program were made by "six [people] in the room at [the] end of the day with two McKinsey consultants," who privileged an outcome-oriented approach.

One Ford respondent reflected on this shift toward a strategic philanthropy mindset:

> *I worry about the direction of philanthropy that it's becoming too strategic in a more business-outcome-oriented sense. I see an awful lot right now of people having goals that seem very egalitarian and very democratic and then shifting into methods for achieving those goals that don't embody those values. . . . If you want a democratic, egalitarian society, [the processes] you engage in themselves should be democratic, egalitarian so that the values you want at the end are also embodied in the work you do.*

Several foundation officials responded to critiques of this nature by pointing to the fact that reform initiatives they pursued were evidence-based, as opposed to simply the "whims" of elites, as one Gates official explained:

> *I think that's why I emphasize the evidence. If it's just "do this" or "do that" and "we're Bill Gates, we're Melinda Gates, we're the Gates Foundation, you should do this," that doesn't fly for me. But when an organization has gone to the trouble of collecting really strong evidence about the needs and about how to address those needs and is willing to put its own resources into this and not just tell people what to do with theirs, that is a very powerful combination.*

Informants at all four foundations made statements that echoed this informant, expressing the value they placed on evidence-based reforms and data-driven practices. For example, at Kellogg, respondents referred to evidence and data as a tool to enable society to function at a "higher level of democracy":

I want foundations to be able to present evidence to people who are making decisions about public resources about effectiveness. That's [philanthropy's] role—if it could somehow do a better job of synthesizing and packaging that learning, that knowledge —that's what it offers society. It's not the resources that are that cool. The unlimited resource here is knowledge. I think that's its mediating role of all of the power behind it. This society needs more data, more knowledge to function at a higher level of democracy right now.

Given how frequently informants spoke about the importance of empirical evidence as a mediating factor in policy influence, it is notable that several respondents also made provocative statements about the dubious nature of the data and research that sometimes guided foundations' decisions. Some argued that this evidence was not always empirically rigorous enough or sponsored by neutral entities. One argued that the evidence that guides foundations, which is often self-funded, may sometimes lack objectivity:

[The foundations are] not putting money in university-based research. They're investing in researchers who are going to do research on their initiatives and who are going to basically do evaluations, not basic research.

A Gates official acknowledged this critique, suggesting that foundation-funded research had the potential to be biased toward a preferred outcome:

It's within [a] sort of fairly narrow orbit that you manufacture the [research] reports. You hire somebody to write a report. There's going to be a commission, there's going to be a lot of research, there's going to be a lot of vetting and so forth and so on, but you pretty much know what the report is going to say before you go through the exercise. I don't think anything overtly nefarious is going on. I just do think this is a sort of a natural function of a set of things that each link in the chain is pretty innocent and it's in isolation and just an accumulation of them adds up.

As an example, the official described Gates's work on value-added teacher assessment and stated that while the initiative had been broadly accepted by professionals with managerial expertise, it lacked substantive critique of its methods and had received insufficient attention to its empirical rigor:

> I've learned to appreciate the output that [consultants] produce, the PowerPoint strategy decks, the way they sort of shape reality to tell a story, [but] it's a very contrived refraction of reality. It poses as data-driven analysis that acts . . . according with a theory of change, and it's going to itself generate evidence and an outcome. . . . Underlying the very solid, conceptually sound notion of strategic grant making lies a lot of rickety data and analysis, so that when you really start to look under the hood on it, it's a far less sound practice than it sounds. The willingness on our part to make stuff up—a lot of it is very ingeniously conceptualized and quasi-analytically derived, but is often very much a hypothesis. . . . [It's] almost always overreaching and ultimately fictional, [and] it takes on a life of its own. In other words, I think it's a sincere self-understanding that's projected outward as a kind of non-ideological pragmatism. You've got a relatively small number of pretty bright and committed people who usually base [decisions] on evidence that, if you look at it carefully, it's dubious. Most good research is usually surrounded by a ton of caveats. So take "value-added"—the best value-added measures we have, the best they can really do is kick out the highest and lowest performers. Everybody else is within the error band. [But] as people get away from technical appendices and the caveats and distill those into summaries and into PowerPoints, into bullet points, and then into data to inform decisions, all that gets washed away and comes back down to sort of what was originally the presupposition you began with, which is "Value-added is the way to evaluate and pay teachers." Because it has a common sense of appeal and it particularly has

a common sense of appeal to a particular mindset and that's, of course, an MBA.

As this interviewee argued, in the field of education philanthropy, the dominance of managerial values inherent in an outcome-oriented approach has become so prevalent as to be nearly taken for granted, echoing broader trends of rationalization across the nonprofit sector.[9] However, the "commonsensical" nature of an outcome-oriented approach tends to elide concerns about top-down reform and power dynamics with grantees, as informants expressed. Thus, foundations' negotiations of these tensions have significant implications not only for the field of education but also for discussions about the broader role of philanthropy in a democratic society.

7

"Should We Critique the Player or the Game Itself?"

Philanthropy and Democracy

B
ehind every managerial question is a normative one, and the variance in foundations' policy-related activities implies different worldviews about the role of foundations in a liberal democracy. Through the lens of an outcome-oriented approach, which primarily values the attainment of effective policy outcomes, foundations should act as effective, efficient problem solvers that can circumvent bureaucratic blockages and catalyze innovation. Through the lens of a field-oriented approach, which primarily values the democratic engagement of citizens, foundations should be vehicles to foster citizenship and mobilize broad political participation. An outcome-oriented approach is often at odds with a field-oriented approach, which results in criticism of foundations that are more prescriptive in their strategies and numerically oriented in their assessment of results. These norms,

according to this argument, may limit democratic participation by privileging the views of elites and may even compromise the benefits that foundations offer in terms of facilitating a variety of voices. However, foundations have been credited with sparking major "wins" in policy, from the civil rights movement to health-care reform—often through providing capital and producing political will that the state cannot.

This tension is at the heart of the recurrent debate that has surrounded foundations over the past century and is rooted in the double-edged sword of foundation accountability to the public. On one hand, foundations are fundamentally private organizations that influence policy priorities outside formal democratic deliberation—a critique that has generated concerns about plutocracy. On the other hand, foundations may benefit democracy as an efficacious alternative to the bureaucratic state. In this argument, foundations sponsor innovation, catalyzing the state to scale promising programs and initiatives, in what Reich characterizes as the "discovery" rationale.[1] Foundations are able to add value because they can move with more agility than government, which is constrained by the voting public.

Instances of discovery rationale permeated interviewees' reflections on foundations in policy. Several referred to the metaphor of "research and development" to describe the benefit of foundations within policy contexts, as one Kellogg official argued:

> *The institution of philanthropy is an incredible resource within American society or global society. It's highly unique and some of the only R&D capital left for social innovation and investing in experiments. It's kind of a do-tank for policy makers to keep their eyes on because there's a lot of good crap that comes out of this.*

In a similar vein, another Kellogg staff member stated:

> *I like the notion that some people call philanthropy the research and development arm of society where it has the luxury and the privilege of being able to explore ideas, test theories, pilot innovation, seed interesting possible change, and it can take a lot of*

*risks that business and government or individuals can't. . . . I
think what's valuable [about] a foundation's role in philanthropy
is [that] they're funding just zillions of different models, in real
settings that really have value because they're worked out in communities where a lot of real social change and innovation does
happen, and they could provide tremendous value in learning for
policy making.*

In addition to their benefits in terms of seeding innovation, foundations also represent a vehicle to support dissent and provide a check
to the state—what Reich terms the "pluralism" rationale.[2] In this vein,
foundations are a critical component of a functional civil society—a
protector of citizen groups that foster democracy. One Ford respondent
described:

*Nonprofit organizations are very important in the voice of Ameri-
can people, often for populations that wouldn't otherwise be heard
by politicians and [administrators]. It's important to us—it's our
mission—to support nonprofit advocacy. Where are organizations
going to get the money to advocate? Most of the time it's from foundations. They're extremely important. A really important role of
funders is to make sure that voices are heard from different actors
and different communities—because I don't know who else will if
they don't.*

In fact, even critics of philanthropy acknowledge foundations' ideal
role as a positive benefit to democracy as a source of funding for policy
innovations, ideas, and initiatives and supporting pluralistic views in
a liberal democracy.[3] One source, a director of a national organization
that advocates for greater foundation accountability, made a statement
that exemplifies this argument:

*I disagree with the solutions that Gates is pushing on education
reform, but I still think it's good for democracy that they're pushing
it. Even though you may not agree with what policy solutions someone is pushing, it's healthy for democracy to have people investing*

*in that and shaking it up. Foundations don't get elected by any-
body, and sometimes it's important to have people that aren't susceptible, don't have to care about getting a profit; they don't have
to care about getting reelected. It's important to have that kind
of freedom sometimes in pushing for things that are unpopular.
Certainly foundations have contributed to some of the great social
movements in our country; if they didn't have the freedom that
they have to operate in these ways, their contributions would not
be as great. Did they cause the civil rights movement? No, the people did. But the money helped.*

This source presents an important but often understated argument:
that even in a well-functioning democracy, the state is constrained by
the median voter and often fails to serve minority preferences that fall
outside of majority interests.[4] Foundations can remedy this failure by
using their power to amplify minority voices, as well as to endorse risk-
ier ventures. Therefore, foundations can use their power to advocate for
competing or unpopular versions of public priorities, acting as a check
on government or as a counterweight to government orthodoxy.

Throughout history, when philanthropy has faced censure for political activity, the pluralism rationale has emerged as a primary justification for foundations' benefit to society. For example, the US Treasury
Report of 1965 argued that foundations were "uniquely qualified to initiate thought and action, experiment with new and untried ventures,
dissent from prevailing attitudes, and act quickly and flexibly," and
concluded that "foundations have enriched the pluralism of our social
order."[5] Simon argues that these positive contributions are possible pre-
cisely because foundations are not accountable: "If private foundations,
as the Treasury wrote in 1965, 'enrich the pluralism of our social order,'
it is largely because the foundations are private, freed from the very
constituent controls that would provide 'accountability.'"[6] Alan Pifer,
then president of the Carnegie Corporation, echoed this language in his
Tax Reform Act hearings testimony in 1969:

It is sad and disturbing to note that some of our critics seem to have so lost faith in foundations and, therefore, in the principle of pluralism in the Nation's life that they appear to favor curtailing the freedom of the very class of tax-exempt institutions whose chief purpose it is to enable pluralism to continue to survive. We trust that these hearings may serve to renew their faith in the American system.[7]

However, this argument has just as frequently been critiqued, as Congresswoman Martha Griffiths evidenced during a sharp rebuke to a foundation official during the Tax Reform Act hearings:

The least of all the arguments and the poorest of all the arguments in my judgment that are being made are the arguments that this charity should be continued and we should have a plural view of charity.[8]

CAN "PLUTOCRATIC" PROCESSES FACILITATE PLURALISM?

Although a number of interviewees acknowledged the important role that foundations could play in facilitating democratic voice, they also, often in the same breath, expressed concern that democratic voice funded by the rich might be "inauthentic," as one respondent characterized, particularly when funds came from larger, more powerful foundations. One respondent argued, "Even if foundations contribute to pluralism, it's still plutocratic pluralism—the pluralism of rich people." Another respondent argued:

The best reason I know of for governments to give people incentives to create and support foundations is to provide plural voices and perspectives. It's far from a perfect strategy because if the voice is louder, the more money you have. I would say that on the whole foundations improve the quality of political discourse compared to what it would be without them. [But I worry about] the more visible and overt [foundations].

Another source echoed this argument:

I am a believer in encouraging a wide variety of initiatives within a society. I don't think relying solely on government structures to do that is a good idea. It is important to have another, as it were, source of initiatives. I believe [foundations] create multiple points of influence; they assure that individuals have ways to support a variety of [views]. [But with] a disproportionately sized [foundation], you create draft, and essentially you help create the problem.

By and large, respondents expressed enthusiasm about the role of foundations in fostering a pluralistic society—up to a point, when the outsize power of some foundations threatened these benefits.[9] One respondent voiced an often-repeated concern: "Scale amplifies everything—Gates dwarfs. No one worries about the influence of [smaller foundations]." Others argued that size itself was not the true concern, but rather the tendency of Gates to concentrate resources in certain spaces—funding a majority of advocacy organizations that addressed teacher quality, for example. One Ford official explained:

Traditionally, [a foundation like Ford] was very diffused. You could say they supported many things in small amounts, and that reduces the danger of domination. Now I think the preference is to become less diverse even internally and just find one or two or three things to focus on and pour all your resources into that effort. So even if you're small, it raises the danger of domination. So it's not necessarily size that matters, it's targeting and focusing on concentration.

NEGOTIATING BETWEEN IMPACT AND LEGITIMACY

Given these complexities, foundations appear to walk a fine line when attempting to influence policy. They are primed to deliver results more quickly than the state, but must also be conscious of appearing to dominate policy debates, for fear of subverting their already contested role in the policy process. Interestingly, a number of interviewees proposed a rationale that seemed to bridge the two approaches: that the democratic engagement of a broad population of citizens actually produces better outcomes. One invoked a combination of rationales to argue that foundations delegate control to grantees rather than retaining it at the foundation level:

> *That's a more effective way to do policy change in philanthropy, and it's a more democratic way to influence policy in philanthropy. It has more people collectively determining what the common good is, as opposed to a few people determining what the common good is. [In the end] you need to have the democratic element to make it stick.*

This argument recalls the trajectory of the Ford Foundation's Gray Areas program in the 1950s and 1960s. Despite Ford's history as a community-focused foundation, critics have argued that the Gray Areas program embodied community engagement principles only rhetorically.[10] The Gray Areas program bore several similarities to Gates's and Broad's current strategies, including operating through closely linked networks between Ford and the government, and focusing on urban environments under executive control. The program was promoted heavily within the networks of policy decision makers, and the federal government committed $30 million to expand Ford's community action projects by 1962 in what was touted as a breakthrough foundation–government partnership.

Nonetheless, the experiments began to falter soon after implementation. Working with ground-level constituents, who had not been involved with the process in a grassroots capacity, proved difficult. The Ford Foundation's model emphasized change through elite connections in a top-down capacity rather than local community organizing, leading to racial tensions between urban residents and the predominantly white, educated administrators who managed the Gray Areas program's on-the-ground intermediary organizations. The Gray Areas program's overemphasis on fast results and elite leadership, at the expense of coalition building with affected constituencies, limited its ultimate reach. O'Connor wrote:

> Committed at least nominally to indigenous participation, Gray Areas was actually far more concerned about making services more comprehensive and efficient than about involving community residents in bringing about reforms. Like the "executive centered" urban mayoralties it funded, the program adopted an unapologetically top-down approach—in which the foundation, and other elite institutions established for the purpose, would act as outside "catalysts" to spark system wide change.[11]

O'Connor argued that the Gray Areas program represented an instance of a top-down intervention as opposed to a bottom-up approach, leading to critique of the program as "a grandiose fusion of paternalism and bureaucracy" due to its inattention to community engagement.[12] Lessons of this nature could be useful for contemporary foundations, yet foundations must also be aware that grassroots approaches are far from a panacea. Foundations that pursue field-oriented strategies will likely face longer timelines in the context of political dynamics that can stymie their efforts and expend resources over the course of years. Additionally, democratic politics are hardly immune from corruption, exclusion, intolerance, and incivility, as Clemens argued: "Even the most participatory organizational structure is not a guarantee that the values and practices advanced by the organization will be consistent with any given understanding of democracy."[13] One respondent agreed, stating:

> I have no illusions that the public system is any more democratic [than philanthropy], given the dominant economic and political patterns in our society. It makes me recall a quotation attributed to Winston Churchill to the effect that democracy is a terrible system, except for all others, which are worse.

Despite the challenges of democratic engagement, active cultivation of broad processes of democratic deliberation represents one of the few mechanisms for foundations to demonstrate their accountability and legitimacy to the broader public. Foundations, particularly those that engage in strategic philanthropy, are particularly susceptible to critiques about their lack of responsibility to the public at large.

One Gates official discussed internal conversations with colleagues on this issue:

> *When we talk about it just amongst colleagues, people come down in a bunch of different places, and I do think it's tricky. You can see stuff go awry. You look at some of the stuff that Ford [and other foundations did decades ago] that turned out badly, and what kind of accountability [do these foundations] have for being a part of a big mess? And the answer is none. We're finding this now [regarding our] accountability versus school boards or mayors or whatever, about who is really accountable to voters and parents around school reform.*

In this vein, another source, a Gates consultant, recalled some of the lessons the foundation learned when it commissioned a report to evaluate one district-level reform initiative. This report concluded that Gates had been a major player in impacting policy changes and also generating some backlash among parent and neighborhood groups. The informant described:

> *No foundation would want to be put in a position where the foundation has come in and it's running things, and it's not accountable and it has this notion of what is right and they've bought the district and the district is going to do. That was a huge lesson. [Gates was] not happy to learn how active they had been [in influencing education policy]. [They did not want to] put themselves in a position where they were seen as attempting to influence a policy context.*

Discussions about foundations' lack of accountability to school districts and distance from the "average citizen," particularly the low-income citizens of color that were often most affected by education reform initiatives, arose in a number of interviews. One grantee of both Gates and Broad explained:

> *A not-insubstantial part of the job is maintaining relationships with program officers. [It's] absolutely crucial. You cannot run a place like this by looking at a website and following grant guidelines. That is in no way the way it works at all. There's a great deal of relationship building. It runs backwards to the way it looks like it runs in a sense that you'll sit down at some point with the right person in the [foundation] and come to some general understanding around money, and then you'll go through the whole formal process of writing up a grant and submitting it.*

This description of the grant-making process suggests that access to funding from foundations, both old and new, is predicated on access to the "right people" through elite networks, and this access is unlikely to be available to an unconnected grassroots organization without the intervention of an elite intermediary. This critique surfaced in the 1969 Tax Reform Act, when Rockefeller board members were tapped to serve in positions in Kennedy's government.[14] These networks between foundations, government, and corporations, shared by virtue of belonging to the same institutions and alma maters and shared governance on corporate boards of directors, form what Nielsen described as an "intricate web" of elite interests that became self-reinforcing over time.[15]

Interviewees echoed this argument, noting that foundations had power to facilitate elite brokerage and bypassed democratic channels due to the greater ease and speed of execution. As one Kellogg official explained: "I'm sitting thinking to myself, I can broker relationships between the people that I've made the grant to and the legislators in such a way that there's an awareness there. And I'm totally going to do it, but I'm just not going to talk about it." Likewise, another respondent reflected on the "soft" channels available to those foundation officials who belonged to elite networks: "Right now the rules say [Gates is] not supposed to be lobbying. Do you think [the foundation is] not lobbying? If I have [an initiative] that's not being approved by [a governmental body], I'd go and talk to the commissioner."

THE PUBLIC IN PRIVATE: ACCOUNTABILITY AND TRANSPARENCY

These informants' remarks underscore the perception of foundations as elite and relatively inaccessible institutions, and throughout their history, foundations have faced numerous calls to be more accountable to the public. Interviewees offered a number of ideas for practical ways in which foundations could increase their accountability. Offering general support grants with core operating support for capacity building and infrastructure, as opposed to project-specific grants, was consistently cited as a best practice in funding, both in terms of effectiveness and democratic inclusiveness.[16] One respondent noted the importance of core support for nonprofit financial survival: "The role of foundations is to build the nonprofit infrastructure. It's so hard for these nonprofits to get operating money." Another respondent voiced a rationale for core support:

> The best way is to give the money to authentic democratic groups on the ground without strings attached. Let them decide what policies to push for and how to push for them. If you give general support grants, you can let the organization itself guide the work.

Interviewees also suggested changes to norms around board governance as a key element in integrating democratic input into foundations' activities. One Ford official explained this rationale, noting the importance of diversifying board representatives to include members from grassroots communities as opposed to solely elites or family members:

> I think you have to start with boards and board governance because foundations are private entities, and they're never going to be fully regulated by government or by civil society pressure.

So I think board diversification, getting more independent repre-sentatives on boards, getting people from the community, people that are actually doing the work on the ground on to boards, and changing their class composition is vital.

Interviewees discussed a number of vehicles for facilitating transparency around foundations' policy-related activities. One called for more public insistence, and perhaps bureaucratic mandate, regarding foundations' disclosure of their activities and openness to public inquiry:

All foundations should be doing evaluations and publishing them for public critique and consumption. Why don't we insist on some independent evaluation of the really big foundations on a long-term basis and present those results for interrogation by members of the public, even by members of Congress? No system of internal accountability or peer pressure is good enough when you have large organizations with large amounts of money. We know that from other sectors.

Others argued that voluntary openness on the part of foundations would likely address a number of concerns about their lack of democratic accountability. One respondent noted:

It's good to have relatively undemocratic sources of initiative, [and] having a broad array of sources of independent funding is probably a good thing, but sunshine is crucial. Independent sources, not directly democratically responsible but open, within some rule of reason in terms of how they operate, [are beneficial]. You ought to be able to see who's doing what [and] where the money is coming from. [It] definitely has to be accountable in the sense of open.

Some respondents pushed back on this idea, however, noting that calls for transparency outside of legal mandates were unenforceable. As one Gates official described: "I don't know how you would regulate it. If you call for transparency there, there's no transparency in the public policy-making process [to begin with]." This interviewee shared an example of working with a superintendent who "played his cards so close to his vest you could read them out his back." A Ford staff member acknowledged this critique, noting that while transparency reforms were "doable technically," they represented a significant challenge politically:

> Think about the huge ruckus that was caused in California by the proposition to just collect diversity data [from foundations]. Foundations fought that tooth-and-nail, even though it was only collecting data. It didn't imply that you actually had to change but, obviously, that was where it was heading in the longer term. So if they fight that, you can imagine the reaction to anything more radical.

These insights suggest that in the absence of formal bureaucratic mechanisms that are designed to ensure greater foundation transparency and accountability, foundations are unlikely to incorporate strategies that reflect these norms. Even if foundations were legally mandated to diversify their boards, accept unsolicited proposals, and allow citizens greater access to their organizations, the likelihood of compliance hardly seems promising, at least within the spirit of the law rather than the letter of the law.

Thus, debates on how to incentivize and ensure foundation transparency continue to be widely debated in the foundation community. Broadly, foundations have responded to calls for greater transparency—at least ceremonially—through annual reports and grant disclosures. However, information regarding the internal operations and decision-making processes of foundations remains relatively limited to the average citizen.[17] As institutions with high barriers to access, foundations have traditionally been perceived as elite institutions that are wary of outsiders. Additionally, foundation offices are often difficult for the public to gain access to, sometimes to the extent that their addresses are unlisted or staff members' names and contact information are not available on websites. Foundations, especially large and prestigious ones, receive volumes of mail, along with inquiries and requests for meetings that require significant time and effort to manage. Institutions with high public profiles also negotiate concerns regarding threats to safety (for example, at an early visit I made to the Gates Foundation, the police were called because an interloper was taking pictures of the foundation building behind multiple security checkpoints and a neighboring building's hedge). However, these elements are also often cited as an expression of foundations' lack of interest in input from the general public.

Some informants rejected the suggestion that foundations should be more democratically operated or inclusive of the public, citing a distinctively American value: the rights of individuals to exercise their personal private property according to their legally protected preferences. One interviewee noted that any further efforts to regulate philanthropy "will be fought like crazy because it will be seen as an unwarranted intervention by the feds and [people will say] 'It's my money and I do what I want with it.'" Others challenged the idea that private wealth was protected, citing a long-standing legal argument that the foundation has some power over foundation resources. The reason is that the charitable tax exemption that foundations benefit from is underwritten by approximately one-third through public funds. One respondent argued:

> *Since this is tax-advantaged money, it's not your money. There's a clear, de facto, philosophical legal argument for requiring more than we currently do of any foundation because otherwise the government would have 33 percent extra resources to spend for itself. Since this is tax-exempt money, we're going to insist on some public involvement in deciding how it's spent.*

Another source, a leader of a regional foundation association, commented on this issue and its potential political implications for foundations, especially during an economic recession:[18]

> *That may be a policy play. There's going to be a US senator that wakes up one day and says, "We've got to look at every tax-privileged dollar there is. Institutional philanthropy is tax privileged. If you*

look at philanthropy, they're really overtly only leveraging 5 percent of those tax-privileged dollars, vis-à-vis this payout thing. Wait a damn minute! What about the other 95 percent? And, hum, this could be a career builder for me," and bingo, you're off to the races.[19]

BIG "P" POLITICS VERSUS LITTLE "P" POLICY

In addition to issues surrounding accountability and transparency, foundations have consistently addressed and challenged regulations on their ability to lobby and advocate. Informants expressed a range of opinions about the regulation and tax treatment of foundations. Outside of formal revision to regulatory measures, respondents voiced a need for expanded education about allowable policy-related activities, including clarifying partisan politics and lobbying as opposed to legally permitted advocacy efforts, as one respondent expressed: "I think that that's an important issue for foundations to think about as they're emerging in this space, that being involved in problem solving is not the same as being involved in partisan politics." One Ford official made the following argument, which was echoed by others:

I'd make a big distinction between what I call big "P" politics and small "p" politics—big "P" meaning partisan engagement, small "p" meaning providing sources for people to have a voice in society in a way that's self-directed. I think there's a slightly murky middle ground between the two poles that I've outlined, which is constantly being explored and pushed by some philanthropists. If you take the Koch brothers on the right or George Soros on the left, they're examples of people who are fairly deliberately pushing the envelope in that middle ground in some fairly partisan directions even though it remains, I think, defensible in small "p" terms.

Others questioned the rationales behind existing regulations on foundation lobbying, noting that restrictions on 501(c)3 public charities and private corporations have significantly loosened, but restrictions on private philanthropy have remained intact since the 1969 hearings. For example, one Gates official argued:

> *If Bill wanted to spend $30 billion of his own money to go lobby, he could. The fact that he could do it personally but now he creates a social institution dedicated to eradicating malaria and improving education for poor children, that that would put restrictions on what he or his funds could do, it seems a little arbitrary.*

Several respondents echoed this perspective, while contrasting the lack of restrictions on corporate lobbying after the Supreme Court's decision on *Citizens United* in 2010, which effectively removed limits on campaign expenditures by private corporations or individuals. A Gates official discussed how the restrictions appeared illogical to many in the foundation world:

> *I think the arguments for the restrictions because of our privileged tax status, that we shouldn't be able to lobby or to electioneer, it seems an odd prohibition. It seems pretty arbitrary to me. I'm not sure, particularly given recent cases in campaign finance, that you'd want to have foundations be out but corporations be in. It just seems like we have this weird patchwork of stuff [to deal with from a regulatory perspective]. If anything, it just makes the money and activity harder to find. It does seem arbitrary and strange because I think, by and large, foundations are "white hat" actors, and have a point of view, but certainly [are] more general interest than Planned Parenthood or the NRA. So it does seem weird that they'd restrict us on it and not them.*

Another Gates source agreed, contrasting the influence of Gates to that of major corporations: "I think while Gates is big and has a big voice, no one in today's world would say that businesses like Exxon don't have a big voice. The idea that there will be undue influence coming from [Gates but not Exxon] seemed a bit ridiculous." Others referenced the restrictions on foundations as a vestige of the 1960s, and that foundations should be considered a legitimate interest group as opposed to operating covertly, as one Gates respondent remarked:

> *I think that the world has changed, and I think that the restrictions that are put on foundations for lobbying are actually too extreme. I mean, when I would meet at the Doubletree Hotel to go out to dinner with a senate education committee member, I couldn't buy her dinner. [And] if we invited elected officials to come to Gates Foundation–issued convenings, we couldn't pay for their hotel rooms. I think foundations should be able to take positions on bills and be considered an interest group and have that be regarded or disregarded at will in the political process. I know that would tarnish to some degree the neutrality and the nonpartisanship that some people view foundations with, but I also think that most foundations that are politically savvy and are active in the political sphere are not really nonpartisan; they're just hiding behind that label.*

Conclusion: Moving the Needle

Given the complex challenges and trade-offs inherent in both outcome-oriented and field-oriented approaches, what is the appropriate role of foundations in the public sphere? Should foundations, like Gates and Broad, that predominantly align with an outcome-oriented approach attempt to integrate aspects of a more field-oriented approach or conclude that democratic deliberation represents a hindrance to achieving effective policy results? Should foundations like Kellogg and Ford, which align more with a field-oriented approach, focus more urgently on achieving calculable impact rather than building fields over the long term? How should foundations interact with public policy—by emphasizing democratic voice for citizens or shaping decision-making processes through elite, expert-driven means? Given the perennial obstacles that face American schools, is democratic engagement justifiable as a first-order priority if an outcome-oriented strategy could potentially create transformative change in public education policy?

Fundamentally, no objective answer to these questions exists. Foundations' differential strategies reflect different value judgments about the appropriate role of private actors in the public realm. At the Tax Reform Act Hearings of 1969, Lawrence Stone, Dean of the UC Berkeley School of Law, argued:

> While it would be comforting to think that there is a "right" and a "wrong" logical answer to such questions, it must be conceded that the answers will, to a significant extent, depend on value judgments. Most important among these are one's views concerning the role of the exempt sector.[20]

I argue that the issue is not whether an outcome-oriented versus field-oriented approach is "right" or "wrong," but that, as informants nearly uniformly argued, the outcome-oriented approach is increasingly viewed as "commonsensical" in the field of education philanthropy, as technological and managerial expertise, with its emphasis on efficiency, effectiveness, and return on investment have become dominant in the field. One Gates informant commented on this development:

> Strategic grant making has this powerful intuitive appeal. The idea that you would not dissipate dollars toward random acts of charity but you would actually try to concentrate dollars in a way that might be a big social return on investment. . . . The education reform landscape or the discourse is really heavily overdetermined by this kind of managerial mindset—a kind of commonsense adaptation to the way companies try to organize to maximize profit. And it's not recognized as actually an ideology in its own right that could compete or that could be challenged by others that could produce data or read data in different ways and draw different inferences. Standards, accountability, capacity building, [they're] commonsensical; you can't quarrel with them. It remains to be seen whether any district can pull this off, but it becomes a sine qua non for getting funding. If you get our money, you'll do it. There's a heavy predisposition to accept the terms.

Paul Brest reflected on the extent to which this approach has become commonplace: "The idea of strategic philanthropy may seem so obvious that there's nothing to write about."[21] Similarly, one Gates official posited, "It seemed like there was still a little talk about field-driven versus strategic grant making ten or fifteen years ago. I know [there are] still a few places here and there that kind of do field-based grant making, but they're pretty few and far between."

These statements about the "common sense," "obvious," and "powerfully intuitive" nature of strategic philanthropy recalls a critique that is frequently invoked by those concerned about foundations' privileged status in the public realm. Karl and Katz explained this critique:

The real success of a particular class's push for societal predominance occurs when it uses its political, moral, and intellectual leadership to articulate a basic world view that subordinate classes come to adopt. This world view becomes . . . the "common sense" of the society. It is accepted as universal and natural, as something of a given, together with the unequal class rule that it legitimates.[22]

Thus, foundations, as elite institutions, use their prestige to validate certain approaches to policy, legitimating social norms and ideologies that become taken for granted and essentially adjudicating between models of social change. Foundations therefore possess a kind of anointing capital that amplifies their financial resources.[23] This is particularly true in policy contexts because they provide the "leverage" that interviewees described as so desirable.[24]

Given the power that foundations possess to shape policies through not only their financial capital, but also their social and political legitimacy, questions of democratic governance come into sharp relief—no longer as a "fringe" critique of socialists, but a matter of great importance to mainstream policy. As Bloomfield commented: "When foundations enter into wholesale public-policy promotion using billions to lure tax-starved districts into scaling up untested models, they have a special obligation to act democratically."[25]

DEEPENING THE DEBATE

How, then, can foundations act more democratically? One Ford source offered a thoughtful response to this perennial question:

> *Part of this is trying to get people to think more rigorously about the conditions under which different approaches to philanthropy are more or less effective and more or less legitimate, and I think if we could get people to be more nuanced in that way, we would realize that there are certain areas where it's fine to take a very directed, top-down, scientific, concentrated approach, and there are other areas where it will be disastrous to do that. People are anxious to find the solution; they think they know what works. They see enemies and opponents and blockages in the system that they want to remove, but [that] gives you no democratic right . . . that's something I think that philanthropists still need to learn.*

"Thinking more rigorously" appears to be easier said than done, however. Multiple informants expressed dissatisfaction with the current level of discourse about normative issues in the field of philanthropy. Several pointed to the role of national professional associations, such as the Council on Foundations (COF) and Independent Sector, in generating more in-depth discussions on these issues. One interviewee related:

> *COF and Independent Sector don't really lead these discussions. COF had nothing to say about this [at a recent conference]. It was all about tax rates—the Foundation Center [too]. All . . . these guys seem to be interested in talking about is how can we fight back against government regulation and how can we get our taxes lower and how can we get still more benefits. They never want to talk about the work. [I want to tell them] "We're so well treated now, lighten up; let's talk about what we're really trying to do," but that's just not the nature of these organizations. It's very frustrating.*

Other interviewees were more forgiving of these organizations' lack of a proactive stance on this issue, noting that the inherent diversity of the philanthropic field meant that professional associations were justifiably reluctant to spearhead a normative conversation, as one stated:

> *I think there really is a diversity among funders, and I think that makes it hard for the field as a whole sometimes to take action . . . they're ideologically totally all over the place. You've met one foundation, you've met one foundation. [They] have to deal with this inconsistency [and qualify internally that] "Oh, this is Broad we're talking to, not Ford." It ultimately makes American philanthropy less of a force as an overall societal entity or resource. Because . . . each one of us has this quirky eclecticism, if you will.*

Another interviewee argued that foundations, as individual institutions, should foster an internal value on debating and discussing their role as policy actors from a critical and historically informed perspective. This interviewee noted that many contemporary program officers are not aware of the issues that inspired the 1969 Tax Reform Act:

> *It's important for folks to remember the context and approach this stuff historically. They work for these foundations, and they don't have a clue what the context is. I think the field suffers badly [from it]. It's the thing foundations most need. Foundations should want to facilitate that debate, to be informed—but they don't. It's appalling. Alas, there is a residual feeling of reluctance to take on any foundation. One of the few accountability mechanisms that exist [is] press and scholarly commentary, but there isn't any critical apparatus. There isn't a body of critical literature.*

Furthermore, critiques of philanthropic involvement in policy have often been expressed using hyperbole, and even the remarks of leading thinkers sometimes tend toward rhetoric of a sensational nature and may be dismissed as partisan or radical as opposed to constructive. Therefore, to move the field of philanthropy past the twin poles of celebration and critique, a measured, intentional, and inclusive discussion about the appropriate role of foundations in influencing public policy must occur—particularly given the contemporary political concerns surrounding income inequality and political influence.

In 2011, when I engaged in initial analyses for this book, I could not have anticipated that a key concern in 2015 would be, instead of the threat of regulation, a much broader critique of income inequality. During several first rounds of interviews in 2011, my informants were relatively dismissive of questions about wealth inequity, which at the time was still viewed as relatively fringe. One source said: "There's worse ways for rich people to spend their money than trying to improve public education; we're lucky that Bill Gates thinks education is important." Another argued: "I think it's tied up with larger ideological questions about the accumulation of wealth. I don't know that the concentration of influence in an institution like a foundation is any better or worse than the vast accumulation of individual wealth, and I don't see Americans looking to take that on."

These respondents, speaking shortly after the denouement of the Occupy Wall Street movement, might be surprised about the extent to which the political tide had turned by 2015, with income inequality emerging as a primary presidential campaign issue, and the Ford Foundation announcing that its entire portfolio would be dedicated to addressing income inequality. In 2015, during a final round of interviews, one former Gates official argued that rather than critiquing foundations as individual institutions, the public should address the underlying institution of philanthropy:

> *Bill and Melinda moved the needle, and I credit them for it. A founder willing to jump in a foxhole and move with urgency— what's wrong with that? The critiques about "Gates treats grantees like contractors" overstate the point, both good and bad. A critique of philanthropy is healthy, but we should make it less about the foundations themselves and more about how influence works. Should we critique the player or the game itself?*

This statement, made just weeks after the Ford Foundation's announcement, underscores the complexity of the questions surrounding the role of philanthropy as a private player in the public arena—and how important this discussion is to US democracy. The system of philanthropy is, at its essence, predicated on and inexorably intertwined with the existence of income inequality in a capitalist system—a fact that, until very recently, has been often overlooked in current dialogue as foundations attempt to ameliorate the effects of poverty and inequality.

Thus, foundations would be wise to devote institutional attention to the consideration of age-old questions about their role in the public realm and to purposefully determine their policy strategies with these normative issues in mind. As Janelle Scott argued, "Foundations must consider the political and philosophical implications of their influence."[26] I add that foundations not only must consider but also actively contribute to recurrent debates in a more audible fashion, treating public concerns about their transparency and accountability seriously, and participating in the democratic process rather than circumventing it. Discussion of the central role that philanthropy plays in policy is a necessity in order to enable the American public to be more critical consumers of reform measures and policies that affect them. Ultimately, this story is crucially important for the practice of philanthropy and the shaping of policy, not just in the field of education, but in numerous fields in which foundations actively attempt to advance social change.

A NOTE ABOUT METHODOLOGY

AN INDUCTIVE APPROACH

When I first became interested in studying philanthropy, I wanted to conduct comparative case studies of several different foundations, an approach that typically requires establishing a specific hypothesis to test and subsequently replicate or disprove. I quickly found, however, that my interests would be better served by using an inductive approach.[1] The inductive approach, sometimes termed interpretive research, explicitly avoids the predefinition of hypotheses but allows the researcher to construct an emerging story as data is compiled, refining inferences and making comparisons along the way. In an interpretive study, the researcher may establish some initial *a priori* assumptions or use a guiding framework to support data collection and analysis. However, the overall process is fundamentally iterative and sensitive to new information; plus, it allows for modification of guiding theories and assumptions accordingly.[2]

Due to the closed nature of the foundation field, I decided I could not establish preexisting hypotheses about the internal norms and workings of foundations, and the inductive approach enabled me to interpret my findings on an emergent basis, often iteratively and in parallel with data collection, to develop theory about how foundations operate from an insider's perspective. Rather than seeking to prove or disprove a theory across different cases, a researcher instead chooses a topic of interest and explores it, allowing the most important themes to arise through carefully executed observations and interviews.

Because of the extreme nature of the foundations studied, as four of the largest private philanthropies in the United States, the findings are not generalizable to foundations more broadly. However, the results represent a revelatory case, using rare data to illuminate an understudied area.[3]

INTERVIEW PROCEDURES

I used both interviews and archival data to cross-validate my findings and determine themes of note, but my primary source of data was semi-structured interviews. To understand how foundations approach policy influence, I required the perspectives of the staff members that negotiated these decisions on a day-to-day basis, and so gaining access to insiders to conduct interviews was a primary consideration—no small task, given this population's high barrier to entry. Weiss states that "the very rich" represent one of the more impenetrable groups of potential respondents in qualitative research, and I might extend his observation by including "those who make decisions regarding the funds of the very rich."[4] To address these concerns, I solicited help in contacting informants from professional and personal contacts, many who have links or past professional experience in these foundations or in the philanthropic field. These orienting figures served as intermediaries who helped me gain inroads into otherwise closed organizations.

The process of soliciting participation from interview subjects often involved multiple channels of communication with different contacts to reach some sources. After the first ten interviews, however, the sample expanded rapidly, as respondents subsequently referred me to their colleagues or professional contacts. To increase access to sources, I guaranteed their anonymity, protecting them from potential professional repercussions. I agreed not to identify them by name or to use details that might disclose their identities. Additionally, instead of recruiting respondents through a central communications or public relations avenue, I solely used unofficial channels in each foundation, relying on individuals who either agreed to speak with me or made credible assurance of my integrity as a researcher to their colleagues.

Between 2010 and 2015, I conducted sixty interviews with sources comprising current and former staff at each of the foundations, influencers in policy and academia, foundation grantees, and practitioners in the broader field of philanthropy. Interviewees were selected to represent roughly structurally equivalent positions in each foundation, including high-level senior staff, education program directors, program officers, and policy officers. In general, I attempt to be as specific as possible in these role descriptions, using actual titles when I can; however, at some foundations, explicitly delineating titles would expose respondents' identities (for example, one foundation's policy and advocacy division was composed of only three people at the time I conducted the interview).

The majority of interviews were conducted in person at locations of the interviewees' choosing, including their offices, local coffee shops, or, in one case, on the floor of the out-of-session state capitol. Interviews averaged approximately sixty minutes in length, and ranged from thirty minutes to two hours. To conduct the interviews, I used several standardized interview protocols, which adjusted to reflect the unique context of each foundation's structure and activities, and contained specific questions depending on the interviewee's role and related expertise.

Because the purpose of the study is to understand the norms that motivate the foundations' policy-related activities, the questions I asked were designed to solicit respondents' interpretations of their foundations' cultures, values, and worldviews. I structured the protocol using guidance from literature on elite interviewing, which is a research technique that is specifically designed for engaging with informants in high-level positions. I structured the interview protocols using a semistructured, open-ended approach rather than a rigid adherence to a script, and vetted the protocol with multiple colleagues prior to conducting interviews, in addition to reviewing foundations' annual reports, press, grant-making patterns, and recent public speeches on record.

ANALYTICAL PROCESS

Immediately following each interview, I followed standardized protocols for protecting confidential data and had the audio files professionally transcribed, which produced approximately two thousand five hundred pages of data.

I initially selected a group of five transcribed interviews and read through them line by line to inductively develop a first round of general "codes," or analytical categories that describe elements that appear in the data. I assigned these codes to highlighted text sections in the initial five transcripts. I then grouped the remainder of the completed transcripts into "families" in qualitative data analysis software, organizing them by the foundation or organization the interviewee represented. I revisited my coding scheme and began a process of more fine-grained coding of transcripts, establishing new codes that emerged from the data *in vivo*. Then I expanded existing codes into more refined and detailed categories, including two or three sublevels, depending on the level of detail that emerged. I coded each family of transcripts separately, coding all the transcripts in a given set before moving on to the next family. As I worked through this process, the coding framework evolved as new codes emerged. Throughout the process of coding, I composed analytic memos that help to contextualize observations within relevant literature, indicate areas for further questioning, and document deviations from previously observed patterns.

After completing the coding for all formal transcribed interviews and the additional notes from five informal interviews, I began the process of developing individual case studies of each foundation, drawing evidence from the interviews as well as archival analysis. To complete these case studies, I reviewed annual reports for each foundation from the last ten years; in addition, I perused websites and conducted LexisNexis searches for major press activity. I also investigated mainstream media and field-specific publications, and read transcripts of relevant speeches made by foundation personnel and field-level actors. I used each foundation's publicly available grants database to review grant-making patterns and priorities related to policy. After completing this archival analysis, I composed descriptive case write-ups of each foundation.

I then began an in-depth process of formulating more complex categories and identifying relationships between the foundations, based on the key concepts and themes that emerged from the data. This process required constant iteration between data and emerging patterns in the findings. Early on in this process of analysis, several broad themes emerged, which provided more opportunities for examining developing inferences as well as discrepant data that emerged. After a number of cycles of focused coding in this manner, I synthesized the themes across the entire corpus of data. Throughout the final document, I edited quotes for readability (redacting words such as *um, you know, sort of,* or pauses that were transcribed verbatim, as well as eliminating duplicative phrases).

APPENDIX

Table of Respondents

Name of organization	Number of interviews	Sample job titles*
Broad Foundation	6	President
Ford Foundation	8	Director Managing Director
Gates Foundation	9	Deputy Director
Kellogg Foundation	10	Senior Director Senior Program Officer Program Officer Senior Policy Officer Policy Officer Communications Manager Communications Officer
Academic researchers	5	Professor
Professional philanthropic associations	6	CEO President Director of Advocacy
Philanthropic consultants	4	Director Senior Advisor Senior Consultant
Grantee organizations	6	Executive Director Analyst Communications Officer
Other foundations	6	President COO CFO General Counsel
Total	60	

*To protect the confidentiality of respondents, details about their divisions and programs (i.e., "Deputy Director of X") have been omitted.

REFERENCES
AND NOTES

CHAPTER 1

Aksartova, Sada. "In Search of Legitimacy: Peace Grant Making of U.S. Philanthropic Foundations, 1988–1996." *Nonprofit and Voluntary Sector Quarterly* 32, no. 1 (2003): 25–46.

Andersen, Brent S. "Foundations as Political Actors: Their Efforts to Shape Interest Group Movements, the Policy-Making Process, and Public Policy Outcomes." Unpublished dissertation. Madison, WI: University of Wisconsin–Madison, 2002.

Bartley, Tim. "How Foundations Shape Social Movements: The Construction of an Organizational Field and the Rise of Forest Certification." *Social Problems* 54, no. 3 (2007): 229–255.

Bernholz, Lucy, Stephanie Linden Seale, and Tony Wang. "Building to Last: Field Building as Philanthropic Strategy." Blueprint Research and Design (2009). http://www.arabellaadvisors.com/wp-content/uploads/2012/03/building-to-last.pdf.

Berry, Jeffrey M. "Nonprofits Shouldn't Be Afraid to Lobby." *Chronicle of Philanthropy.* November 27, 2003.

Berry, Jeffrey, and David Arons. *A Voice for Nonprofits.* Washington, DC: Brookings Institution, 2005.

Bothwell, Robert. "Up Against Conservative Public Policy: Alternatives to Mainstream Philanthropy." In *Foundations for Social Change: Critical Perspectives on Philanthropy and Popular Movements,* edited by Daniel Faber and Deborah McCarthy, 115–150. Lanham, MD: Rowman and Littlefield, 2005.

Bremner, Robert H. *American Philanthropy.* Chicago, IL: University of Chicago Press, 1988.

Brody, Evelyn, and John E. Tyler. "Respecting Foundation and Charity Autonomy: How Public Is Private Philanthropy?" *Chicago-Kent Law Review* 85, no. 2 (2010): 571–617.

Carr, Patrick Joseph. "Private Voices, Public Forces: Agenda Setting and the Power of Foundations in the NCLB Era." Unpublished dissertation. Washington, DC: Georgetown University, 2012.

Cohen, Rick. "Philanthropic World Voices Mixed Reaction on Buffett's Gift to Gates Fund." *Chronicle of Philanthropy.* July 20, 2006.

Colwell, Mary Anna Culleton. *Private Foundations and Public Policy: The Political Role of Philanthropy.* New York, NY: Garland Publishing, 1993.

Commission on Industrial Relations. "Final Report and Testimony Submitted to Congress." 1916.

Covington, Sally. "Right Thinking, Big Grants, and Long-Term Strategy: How Conservative Philanthropies and Think Tanks Transform US Public Policy." *Covert Action Quarterly* 63 (1998): 1–8.

Cuninggim, Merrimon. *Private Money and Public Service: The Role of Foundations in American Society.* 1st ed. New York, NY: McGraw-Hill Education, 1972.

Edie, John. "A Lift for Lobbying." *Foundation News* 32, no. 2 (1991): 40–45.

Faber, Daniel, and Deborah McCarthy (eds.). *Foundations for Social Change: Critical Perspectives on Philanthropy and Popular Movements.* Lanham, MD: Rowman and Littlefield, 2005.

Ferris, James M., Guilbert C. Hentschke, and Hilary Joy Harmssen. "Philanthropic Strategies for School Reform." *Educational Policy* 22, no. 5 (2008): 705–730.

Ferris, James M., and Michael Mintrom. *Foundations and Public Policymaking: A Conceptual Framework.* Los Angeles, CA: Center on Philanthropy and Public Policy, University of Southern California, 2002.

Fleishman, Joel L. *The Foundation: A Great American Secret.* New York, NY: PublicAffairs, 2009.

Fremont Smith, Marion R. *Governing Nonprofit Organizations: Federal and State Law and Regulations.* Cambridge, MA: Harvard University Press, 2004.

Frumkin, Peter. "Accountability and Legitimacy in American Foundation Philanthropy." In *The Legitimacy of Philanthropic Foundations,* edited by Kenneth Prewitt, Mattei Dogan, Steven Heydemann, and Stefan Toepler, 99–122. New York, NY: Russell Sage Foundation, 2006.

———. "The Long Recoil from Regulation: Private Philanthropic Foundations and the Tax Reform Act of 1969." *The American Review of Public Administration* 28, no. 3 (1998): 266–286.

———. *Trouble in Foundationland: Looking Back, Looking Ahead.* Washington, DC: Hudson Institute, 2004. http://www.hudson.org/content/researchattachments/attachment/1251/frumkin_2004_pdf.pdf.

Gallagher, Karen Symms, and Jerry D. Bailey. "The Politics of Teacher Education Reform: Strategic Philanthropy and Public Policy Making." *Educational Policy* 14, no. 1 (2000): 11–24.

Haines, Herbert. *Black Radicals and the Civil Rights Mainstream, 1954–1970.* Knoxville, TN: University of Tennessee Press, 1988.

Hall, Peter Dobkin. "A Historical Overview of Philanthropy, Voluntary Associations, and Nonprofit Organizations in the United States." In *The Nonprofit Sector: A Research Handbook.* 2nd ed., edited by Walter W. Powell and Richard Steinberg, 32–65. New Haven, CT: Yale University Press, 2006.

———. "A Historical Overview of the Private Nonprofit Sector." In *The Nonprofit Sector: A Research Handbook.* 1st ed., edited by Walter W. Powell and Richard Steinberg, 3–26. New Haven, CT: Yale University Press, 1987.

Hammack, David C. "American Debates on the Legitimacy of Foundations." In *The Legitimacy of Philanthropic Foundations*, edited by Kenneth Prewitt, Mattei Dogan, Steven Heydemann, and Stefan Toepler, 49–98. New York, NY: Russell Sage Foundation Publications, 2006.

Heimann, Fritz. *The Future of Foundations*. Saddle River, NJ: Prentice Hall, 1973.

Hoffman, Nancy, and Robert Schwartz. "Foundations and School Reform: Bridging the Cultural Divide." In *Reconnecting Education and Foundations*, edited by Ray Bacchetti and Thomas Ehrlich, 107–138. San Francisco, CA: Jossey-Bass, 2007.

Hwang, Hokyu, and Walter W. Powell. "The Rationalization of Charity: The Influences of Professionalism in the Nonprofit Sector." *Administrative Science Quarterly* 54, no. 2 (2009): 268–298.

Jenkins, J. Craig. "Resource Mobilization Theory and the Study of Social Movements." *Annual Review of Sociology* 9 (1983): 527–553.

———. "Channeling Social Protest: Foundation Patronage of Contemporary Social Movements." In *Private Action and the Public Good*, edited by Walter W. Powell and Elisabeth S. Clemens, 206–216. New Haven, CT: Yale University Press, 1998.

Jenkins, J. Craig, and Craig Eckert. "Channeling Black Insurgency: Elite Patronage and the Development of the Civil Rights Movement." *American Sociological Review* 51 no. 6 (1986): 812–830.

Jenkins, J. Craig, and Abigail Halcli. "Grassrooting the System? The Development and Impact of Social Movement Philanthropy, 1953–1990." In *Philanthropic Foundations, New Scholarship, New Possibilities*, edited by Ellen Condliffe Lagemann, 229–256. Bloomington, IN: Indiana University Press, 1999.

Karl, Barry D., and Stanley N. Katz. "The American Private Philanthropic Foundation and the Public Sphere 1890–1930." *Minerva* 19, no. 2 (1981): 236–270.

———. "Foundations and Ruling Class Elites." *Daedalus* 116, no. 1 (1987): 1–40.

Kohl-Arenas, Erica. *The Self-Help Myth: How Philanthropy Fails to Alleviate Poverty*. Berkeley, CA: University of California Press, 2015.

Kronley, Robert A., and Claire Handley. *Maturing Investments: Philanthropy and Middle Grades Reform*. Atlanta, GA: Kronley & Associates, 2003. http://www.kronley.com/documents/MaturingInvestments-Clark.pdf.

Lagemann, Ellen Condliffe. *Private Power for the Public Good: A History of the Carnegie Foundation for the Advancement of Teaching*. Middletown, CT: Wesleyan University Press, 1983.

———. *The Politics of Knowledge: The Carnegie Corporation, Philanthropy, and Public Policy*. Chicago, IL: University of Chicago Press, 1989.

Marris, Peter, and Martin Rein. *Dilemmas of Social Reform: Poverty and Community Action in the United States*. Chicago, IL: University of Chicago Press, 1973.

Mavity, Jane H., and Paul N. Ylvisaker. "Private Philanthropy and Public Affairs." In *Research Papers Sponsored by the Private Philanthropy and Public Needs*, vol. 2, 795–836. Washington, DC: US Department of the Treasury, 1977.

McCarthy, John D. and Mayer Zald. "Resource Mobilization and Social Movements: A

Partial Theory." *American Journal of Sociology*, 82, no. 6 (1977): 1212–1241.

McKersie, William S. "Strategic Philanthropy and Local Public Policy: Lessons from Chicago School Reform, 1987–1993." Unpublished dissertation. Chicago, IL: University of Chicago, 1998.

Nagai, Althea, Robert Lerner, and Stanley Rothman. *The Culture of Philanthropy: Foundations and Public Policy*. Washington, DC: Capital Research Center, 1991.

Nielsen, Waldemar A. *The Big Foundations*. New York, NY: Columbia University Press, 1972.

O'Connor, Alice. "The Ford Foundation and Philanthropic Activism in the 1960s." In *Philanthropic Foundations: New Scholarship, New Possibilities*, edited by Ellen Condliffe Lagemann, 169–194. Bloomington, IN: Indiana University Press, 1999.

Ostrander, Susan A. "Legacy and Promise for Social Justice Funding: Charitable Foundations and Progressive Social Movements, Past and Present." In *Foundations for Social Change: Critical Perspectives on Philanthropy and Popular Movements*, edited by Daniel Faber and Deborah McCarthy, 33–60. Lanham, MD: Rowman & Littlefield, 2005.

Ostrower, Francie. *Attitudes and Practices Concerning Philanthropy*. Washington, DC: The Urban Institute Center on Nonprofits and Philanthropy, 2004.

Piven, Frances Fox, and Richard Cloward. *Poor People's Movements: Why They Succeed, How They Fail*. New York: Pantheon Books, 1977.

Quinn, Rand, Megan Tompkins-Stange, and Debra Meyerson. "Beyond Grantmaking: Philanthropic Foundations as Agents of Change and Institutional Entrepreneurs." *Nonprofit and Voluntary Sector Quarterly* 43, no. 6 (2014): 950–968.

Reckhow, Sarah. *Follow the Money: How Foundation Dollars Change Public School Politics*. New York, NY: Oxford University Press, 2013.

Rich, Andrew. *Think Tanks, Public Policy, and the Politics of Expertise*. Cambridge, UK: Cambridge University Press, 2004.

Roelofs, Joan. *Foundations and Public Policy: The Mask of Pluralism*. Albany, NY: State University of New York Press, 2003.

———. "Liberal Foundations: Impediments or Supports for Social Change?" In *Foundations for Social Change: Critical Perspectives on Philanthropy and Popular Movements*, edited by Daniel Faber and Deborah McCarthy, 61–88. Lanham, MD: Rowman & Littlefield, 2005.

Scott, Janelle. "The Politics of Venture Philanthropy in Charter School Policy and Advocacy." *Educational Policy* 23, no. 1 (2009): 106–136.

Scott, Janelle, and Huriya Jabbar. "The Hub and the Spokes: Foundations, Intermediary Organizations, Incentivist Reforms, and the Politics of Research Evidence." *Educational Policy* 28, no. 2 (2014): 233–257.

Sealander, Judith. "Curing Evils at Their Source: The Arrival of Scientific Giving." In *Charity, Philanthropy and Civility in American History*, edited by Lawrence J. Friedman and Mark D. McGarvie, 217–239. Cambridge, UK: Cambridge University Press, 2003.

————. *Private Wealth and Public Life: Foundation Philanthropy and the Reshaping of American Social Policy from the Progressive Era to the New Deal.* Baltimore, MD: Johns Hopkins University Press, 1997.

Sievers, Bruce R. "Eight Questions Reporters Should've Asked About the Buffett Donation." *Stanford Social Innovation Review,* November 28, 2006.

Simon, John, Harvey Dale, and Laura Chisolm. "Federal Tax Treatment of Charitable Organizations." In *The Nonprofit Sector: A Research Handbook.* 2nd ed. edited by Walter W. Powell and Richard Steinberg, 267–306. New Haven, CT: Yale University Press, 2006.

Simon, John G. "Foundations and Public Controversy: An Affirmative View." In *The Future of Foundations,* edited by Fritz F. Heimann, 58–100. Saddle River, NJ: Prentice Hall, 1973.

————. "The Regulation of American Foundations: Looking Backward at the Tax Reform Act of 1969." *Voluntas* 6, no. 3 (1995): 243–254.

Smith, James Allen. *Foundations and Public Policymaking: A Historical Perspective.* Los Angeles, CA: Center on Philanthropy and Public Policy, University of Southern California, 2002.

Snyder, Jeffrey W. "How Old Foundations Differ from New Foundations." In *The New Education Philanthropy: Politics, Policy, and Reform,* edited by Frederick M. Hess and Jeffrey Henig, 29–54. Cambridge, MA: Harvard Education Press, 2015.

Teles, Steven M. *The Rise of the Conservative Legal Movement: The Battle for Control of the Law.* Princeton, NJ: Princeton University Press, 2008.

Troyer, Thomas A. "The 1969 Private Foundation Law: Perspective on Its Origins and Underpinnings." *The Exempt Organization Tax Review* 27, no. 1 (2000): 52–65.

Walsh, Frank. "Perilous Philanthropy." *The Independent* LXXXIII, July–September (1915): 262.

Weaver, Warren, and George Wells Beadle. *U.S. Philanthropic Foundations: Their History, Structure, Management, and Record.* New York: Harper and Row, 1967.

Weinryb, Noomi. "The Policy Paradox of Philanthropy: Accountability Mechanisms, Legitimacy and Policy Influence." Paper presented at the 38th Annual Meeting of the Association for Research on Nonprofit Organizations and Voluntary Action, Cleveland, OH, November 19–21, 2009.

Zunz, Olivier. *Philanthropy in America: A History.* Princeton, NJ: Princeton University Press, 2011.

1. Francie Ostrower, *Attitudes and Practices Concerning Philanthropy* (Washington, DC: The Urban Institute Center on Nonprofits and Philanthropy, 2004).

2. Joel L. Fleishman, *The Foundation: A Great American Secret* (New York: PublicAffairs, 2009).

3. Noomi Weinryb, "The Policy Paradox of Philanthropy: Accountability Mechanisms, Legitimacy and Policy Influence." (Paper presented at the 38th Annual

Meeting of the Association for Research on Nonprofit Organizations and Voluntary Action, Cleveland, OH, November 19–21, 2009).

4. Bruce R. Sievers, "Eight Questions Reporters Should've Asked About the Buffett Donation," *Stanford Social Innovation Review*, November 28, 2006.

5. Rick Cohen, "Philanthropic World Voices Mixed Reaction on Buffett's Gift to Gates Fund," *Chronicle of Philanthropy*, July 20, 2006.

6. Nancy Hoffman and Robert Schwartz, "Foundations and School Reform: Bridging the Cultural Divide," in *Reconnecting Education and Foundations*, ed. Ray Bacchetti and Thomas Ehrlich (San Francisco, CA: Jossey-Bass, 2007), 107–138.

7. Judith Sealander, "Curing Evils at Their Source: The Arrival of Scientific Giving," in *Charity, Philanthropy and Civility in American History*, ed. Lawrence J. Friedman and Mark D. McGarvie (Cambridge, UK: Cambridge University Press, 2003), 217–239.

8. See, for example, James M. Ferris, Guilbert C. Hentschke, and Hilary Joy Harmssen, "Philanthropic Strategies for School Reform," *Educational Policy* 22, no. 5 (2008): 705–730; Janelle Scott, "The Politics of Venture Philanthropy in Charter School Policy and Advocacy," *Educational Policy* 23, no. 1 (2009): 106–136; Patrick Joseph Carr, "Private Voices, Public Forces: Agenda Setting and the Power of Foundations in the NCLB Era" (Unpublished dissertation, Washington, DC: Georgetown University, 2011); Sarah Reckhow, *Follow the Money: How Foundation Dollars Change Public School Politics* (New York, NY: Oxford University Press, 2013); Rand Quinn, Megan Tompkins-Stange, and Debra Meyerson, "Beyond Grantmaking: Philanthropic Foundations as Agents of Change and Institutional Entrepreneurs," *Nonprofit and Voluntary Sector Quarterly* 43, no. 6 (2014): 950–968; Janelle Scott and Huriya Jabbar, "The Hub and the Spokes: Foundations, Intermediary Organizations, Incentivist Reforms, and the Politics of Research Evidence," *Educational Policy* 28, no. 2 (2014): 233–257; Erica Kohl-Arenas, *The Self-Help Myth: How Philanthropy Fails to Alleviate Poverty* (Berkeley, CA: University of California Press, 2015).

9. Mary Anna Culleton Colwell, *Private Foundations and Public Policy: The Political Role of Philanthropy* (New York, NY: Garland Publishing, 1993); William S. McKersie, "Strategic Philanthropy and Local Public Policy: Lessons from Chicago School Reform, 1987–1993" (Unpublished dissertation, Chicago, IL: University of Chicago, 1998).

10. Jane H. Mavity and Paul N. Ylvisaker, "Private Philanthropy and Public Affairs," in *Research Papers Sponsored by the Private Philanthropy and Public Needs* (Washington, DC: US Department of the Treasury, 1977): 795–836; Peter Dobkin Hall, "A Historical Overview of the Private Nonprofit Sector," in *The Nonprofit Sector: A Research Handbook*, 1st ed., ed. Walter W. Powell and Richard Steinberg (New Haven, CT: Yale University Press, 1987), 3–26; Evelyn Brody and John E. Tyler, "Respecting Foundation and Charity Autonomy: How Public Is Private Philanthropy?", *Chicago-Kent Law Review* 85, no. 2 (2010): 571–617.

11. Tim Bartley, "How Foundations Shape Social Movements: The Construction of

an Organizational Field and the Rise of Forest Certification," *Social Problems* 54, no. 3 (2007): 229–255; Hokyu Hwang and Walter W. Powell, "The Rationalization of Charity: The Influences of Professionalism in the Nonprofit Sector," *Administrative Science Quarterly* 54, no. 2 (2009): 268–298; Quinn, Tompkins-Stange, and Meyerson, "Beyond Grantmaking: Philanthropic Foundations as Agents of Change and Institutional Entrepreneurs," 950–968.

12. Barry D. Karl and Stanley N. Katz, "Foundations and Ruling Class Elites," *Daedalus* 116, no. 1 (1987): 1–40.

13. Peter Dobkin Hall, "A Historical Overview of Philanthropy, Voluntary Associations, and Nonprofit Organizations in the United States," in *The Nonprofit Sector: A Research Handbook*, 2nd ed., ed. Walter W. Powell and Richard Steinberg (New Haven, CT: Yale University Press, 2006), 32–65; Olivier Zunz, *Philanthropy in America: A History* (Princeton, NJ: Princeton University Press, 2012).

14. Sealander, "Curing Evils at Their Source: The Arrival of Scientific Giving," 217–239.

15. Think tanks have traditionally been a preferred vehicle of foundations that fund intellectual capital with the intent of influencing policy. According to Rich (2004), foundations recognized early on that "experts are political actors, and think tanks are among the most active and efficient expert political institutions" (205). Rich details the central role of policy experts and research conducted in think tanks in injecting ideas into political debate. Originally, think tanks appealed to foundations due to their emphasis on cultivating scholars to develop policy platforms and ideas that could be circulated to policy makers to influence the agenda-setting process of policy deliberation. In the 1950s, for example, the Ford Foundation was a primary supporter of think tanks as part of a larger program designed to fund "knowledge-creating institutions" (61). Rich argues that large private foundations like Ford were the primary source of funding for think tanks until the 1960s, as these funders "appreciated, even encouraged, the detached and neutral efforts of think tanks" (205). Teles (2008) describes how in the 1960s, as Ford's agenda became more activist in nature, it began to diversify its funding to make grants not only to research-oriented think tanks but also to advocacy organizations that could help frame and disseminate the knowledge capital that was produced. These efforts became part of a broader effort to build a field infrastructure to accomplish progressive change, which a number of liberal foundations pursued by funding think tanks, universities, and advocacy organizations. By building what Teles terms a "liberal legal network" (22), these networked foundations intended to entrench civil rights values in public policy. Teles illustrates the activist culture of the Ford Foundation under McGeorge Bundy (former National Security Advisor to Presidents Kennedy and Johnson from 1961 to 1966 prior to assuming the Ford Foundation's presidency) in the late 1960s: "The Ford Foundation had been involved in legal reform for more than a decade, but with Bundy's rise, the foundation's leadership and its work in the area became much more ambitious and far-reaching" (35). In addition to its funding of research and knowledge-building,

Ford cultivated relationships with elite academic institutions to develop clinical education programs and public interest law firms to provide legal representation to underserved populations. Roelofs (2005) describes the impact of investments in clinical legal education as having a profound effect on Supreme Court–based decision making—the "network of institutions and policy oriented law reviews was a feeder to rights-based litigation" (67). Its direct policy efforts involved a strategic initiative to "seed litigation"—playing a central role in "selecting, coordinating, and financing significant test cases likely to establish fundamental precedents in remedying injustices and enhancing the rights and opportunities of the poor" (Teles, 34). In the decades following this effort in the 1960s, a number of think tanks began to become more politically partisan and visible, shifting from producing objective research to more ideological research. In addition, they began to work in concert with field-level advocacy organizations to develop a coherent political agenda and support media institutions as vehicles for dissemination, reflecting a shift toward a market-based orientation. This model attracted a different type of funder, and conservative foundations such as Bradley, Earhart, Carthage, Olin, and Scaife were particularly supportive of this approach (Covington, 1998; Rich, 2004). These foundations invested significant resources in developing institutions that cultivated intellectual capital in an attempt to counteract the rise of progressive policy in the late 1960s (Teles, 2008). In fact, Ford's efforts to establish a progressive field of organizations devoted to legal system reform spurred a conservative countermovement against the rise of liberal policy during the 1960s, as a cohort of foundations coordinated grant making to a group of think tanks with the explicit purpose of disseminating conservative values into public policy (Covington, 1998; Rich, 2004; Teles, 2008). In contrast to the earlier funding of think tanks to produce "objective" social science research, this strategy funded research that reflected partisan ideas, such as market-oriented values, and worked with advocacy organizations to disseminate policy ideas. Conservative foundations thus built a national organizing structure around linked institutions (such as think tanks, lobbying organizations, and media outlets) (Covington, 1998; Smith, 2002).

16. Ellen Condliffe Lagemann, *The Politics of Knowledge: The Carnegie Corporation, Philanthropy, and Public Policy*, 1st ed. (Chicago, IL: University of Chicago Press, 1989); Karen Symms Gallagher and Jerry D. Bailey, "The Politics of Teacher Education Reform: Strategic Philanthropy and Public Policy Making," *Educational Policy* 14, no. 1 (2000): 11–24; Sada Aksartova, "In Search of Legitimacy: Peace Grant Making of U.S. Philanthropic Foundations, 1988–1996," *Nonprofit and Voluntary Sector Quarterly* 32, no. 1 (2003): 25–46; Andrew Rich, *Think Tanks, Public Policy, and the Politics of Expertise* (Cambridge, UK: Cambridge University Press, 2004); James Allen Smith, "Foundations and Public Policymaking: A Historical Perspective" (Los Angeles, CA: Center on Philanthropy and Public Policy, University of Southern California, 2002).

17. Lagemann's (1989) analysis describes how the Carnegie Corporation "quietly but effectively use[d] power and private money to influence public policies" through

supporting the development of specific types of social science expertise that were used to inform policy makers about policy changes. Lagemann examines how, as data and social science became important tools to address social ills during the Progressive Era, knowledge and expertise became "more and more essential to economic activity and to the formulation, implementation, and evaluation of public policy" (4). Lagemann illustrates how the Carnegie Corporation capitalized on this demand by adjudicating the types of knowledge that would be considered legitimate in policy discussions, in areas such as education and the social sciences. It also sponsored several groundbreaking studies designed to support liberal public policy and develop institutions to position the foundation as an arbiter of expertise for policy makers, as well as to cultivate the institutions that would help to produce this knowledge, in order to be positioned to inform policy decisions. Among its activities, Carnegie sponsored Gunnar Myrdal's 1944 work, *An American Dilemma: The Negro Problem and Modern Democracy*, which was credited as a major influence in the 1954 US Supreme Court decision in *Brown v. Board of Education*. Carnegie's efforts in advancing social science work and knowledge-building institutions were mirrored by their investments in elevating university-based scientific expertise as the professional standard in fields such as medicine. Gallagher and Bailey (2000) describe how the Carnegie Corporation was also influential in professionalizing medical education in the early twentieth century as part of an effort to hold higher education institutions to elevated standards of scientific expertise. Carnegie commissioned the Flexner Report, which investigated subpar medical training and admission standards at proprietary and osteopathic medical schools. The Flexner Report developed specific standards for all medical schools to adopt, and they were endorsed by professional medical associations. As a result, more than half of nonuniversity medical programs closed within ten years of the report's completion. The effort to professionalize medical education was one of the first components of Carnegie's broader strategy to influence policy through legitimizing specific types of expertise and knowledge.

18. Kronley and Handley (2003) describe how in the 1990s, the Carnegie Corporation played a central role in advancing education reform by making grants to fifteen states through the Middle Grade Schools State Policy Initiative. The purpose of these grants was to facilitate states' development of "policies to promote middle grades reform and supporting middle schools in those states and communities that were committed to and working toward reform" (32). The initiative's early efforts focused on working with states to develop policies around middle schools; it funded the development of task forces and other convening mechanisms toward the goal of raising awareness and using evidence of best practices in policy formulation. Kronley and Handley regard this initiative as influential and far-reaching in its impact, noting that Carnegie played a central role not only in developing its own programs but also in making connections with other on-the-ground organizations that worked for similar goals, which helped build more local capacity

and support. Kronley and Handley note, "Carnegie...generated a momentum for reform that would likely have been lacking in its absence" (28). Later in the 1990s, Carnegie revised the initiative to fund demonstration projects of networks of exemplar schools.

19. Sealander, "Curing Evils at Their Source: The Arrival of Scientific Giving," 217–239.

20. Peter Marris and Martin Rein, *Dilemmas of Social Reform: Poverty and Community Action in the United States* (Chicago, IL: University of Chicago Press, 1973); Alice O'Connor, "The Ford Foundation and Philanthropic Activism in the 1960s," in *Philanthropic Foundations: New Scholarship, New Possibilities*, ed. Ellen Condliffe Lagemann (Bloomington, IN: Indiana University Press, 1999), 169–194.

21. O'Connor , "The Ford Foundation and Philanthropic Activism in the 1960s," 176.

22. O'Connor, "The Ford Foundation and Philanthropic Activism in the 1960s," 169–194; Joan Roelofs, "Liberal Foundations: Impediments or Supports for Social Change?", in *Foundations for Social Change: Critical Perspectives on Philanthropy and Popular Movements*, ed. Daniel Faber and Deborah McCarthy (Lanham, MD: Rowman & Littlefield, 2005), 61–88; Steven M. Teles, *The Rise of the Conservative Legal Movement: The Battle for Control of the Law* (Princeton, NJ: Princeton University Press, 2008).

23. During this period, Ford began experimenting with demonstration projects designed to address urban social deterioration. O'Connor (1999) emphasizes that Ford was not the first foundation to become involved in public policy, but that it represented a sharp departure in its approach from "associational" to "activist" (170). After World War II, rapidly changing social dynamics, such as expanding social welfare programs, opened up new opportunities for policy experimentation. In the late 1940s, the expansion of social welfare programs represented opportunities for foundations to work with government agencies to implement new models of service delivery. In 1955, the program's director, Paul Ylvisaker, determined that Ford's Gray Areas program would depart from traditional "philanthropic detachment" by helping "create the new institutional forms that would make government work" (176). Ford created intermediary organizations to coordinate work and grants in inner cities, aggressively promoted the Gray Areas program within networks of policy makers, many of whom were former Ford Foundation staff members or consultants, and the use of research to identify potential areas of direct social impact. While the government committed $30 million to the project in 1962, the experiments began to falter soon after implementation. The Ford Foundation still claimed the Gray Areas program as a success, especially since its models were integrated into the Economic Opportunity Act of 1964 (O'Connor, 1999).

24. Teles, *The Rise of the Conservative Legal Movement: The Battle for Control of the Law*, 20.

25. O'Connor, "The Ford Foundation and Philanthropic Activism in the 1960s," 169–194.

26. See, for example, Warren Weaver and George Wells Beadle, *U.S. Philanthropic Foundations: Their History, Structure, Management, and Record* (New York, NY:

Harper and Row, 1967); Barry D. Karl and Stanley N. Katz, "The American Private Philanthropic Foundation and the Public Sphere 1890–1930," *Minerva* 19, no. 2 (1981): 236–270; Robert H. Bremner, *American Philanthropy* (Chicago, IL: University of Chicago Press, 1988); Peter Frumkin, "Accountability and Legitimacy in American Foundation Philanthropy," in *The Legitimacy of Philanthropic Foundations*, ed. Kenneth Prewitt, et al. (New York, NY: Russell Sage Foundation, 2006), 99–122; David C. Hammack, "American Debates on the Legitimacy of Foundations," in *The Legitimacy of Philanthropic Foundations*, ed. Kenneth Prewitt, et al. (New York, NY: Russell Sage Foundation, 2006), 49–98; Robert Reich, "What Are Foundations For?", *Boston Review*, March 1, 2013, http://www.bostonreview.net/forum/what-are-foundations/policy-advocates.

27. Walsh, "Perilous Philanthropy," 1916.

28. John G. Simon, "The Regulation of American Foundations: Looking Backward at the Tax Reform Act of 1969," *Voluntas* 6, no. 3 (1995): 243–254.

29. Merrimon Cuninggim, *Private Money and Public Service: The Role of Foundations in American Society*, 1st ed. (New York, NY: McGraw-Hill Education, 1972).

30. H.R. 13270 represented an unprecedented movement by the federal government into the regulatory territory of states. According to Fremont Smith (2004, 377), the federal government's powers "expanded so that it is effectively the primary source of regulation, extending to matters that had previously been the exclusive province of the state and, in many instances, preempting state regulation by conditioning tax exemption upon compliance with federal standards of behavior." Simon (1995) emphasizes the importance of the federal government's decision to assume a role overseeing private foundations, stating that "state courts of equity and attorneys general are more accustomed to dealing with the policing of fiduciary that is the federal tax system . . . most of the 1969 congressional targets . . . involve fiduciary issues that are the meat and drink of state regulators" (247). In a debate with Treasury officials in 1966, Simon (1995) notes that he recommended that the states, rather than the federal government, set their own regulations on foundations, but found that this proposal was "met with scorn" (247). Additionally, many of the penalties against foundations were unprecedented constitutionally; for example, no legal precedent existed for the federal government to impose excise taxes (Simon, 1995).

31. The major provisions of the Tax Reform Act included a ban on self-dealing, or entering into business transactions while representing the foundation; taxation on income from investments; limitation of excess business holdings or ownership of corporations, to 20 percent; a mandated annual endowment payout requirement of 6 percent (later reduced to 5 percent); requirements for public disclosure of funding activities; and limitations on advocacy activities. Prior to the Tax Reform Act's adoption, guidelines had already been established, albeit ambiguous ones, about nonprofits' allowable political behavior. The Revenue Act of 1934 placed basic limitations on 501(c)3 lobbying, stating that nonprofit organizations

could not engage in a "substantial" amount of lobbying, while leaving the definition of "substantial" unclear. Scholars argue that the justification for the stricter measures for foundations "rested on no stated ground not equally applicable to public charities" (Troyer, 2000, 64). Simon, Dale, and Chisholm (2006) state that "no cogent, consistent rationale for the various restrictions on political activity . . . can be unearthed in the legislative record of their enactment" (285). Instead, these restrictions were "adopted piecemeal, often with little discussion, and, in the case of the campaigning ban, as an apparently ad hoc response to a perceived affront to the lawmakers who sponsored the bill" (286). In 1974, Congress sought to amend the law in the face of criticism about its "excessive and pernicious" measures (Berry, 2003, 3), and liberalized the tax regulations that applied to public charities. These reforms, introduced in 1976, included an option for public charities to elect a so-called 501(h) designation, which specified allowable lobbying activities as a percentage of an organization's expenses, as opposed to the previous "substantial" standard (Berry and Arons, 2003; Simon, Dale, and Chisholm, 2006). No such "statutory clarification" applied to foundations, however; according to Troyer (2000, 64), Congress "[took] pains . . . to point out that the liberalization was not to apply to private foundations."

32. Simon, "The Regulation of American Foundations: Looking Backward at the Tax Reform Act of 1969," 243–254; Thomas A. Troyer, "The 1969 Private Foundation Law: Perspective on Its Origins and Underpinnings," *The Exempt Organization Tax Review* 27, no. 1 (2000): 52–65; Jeffrey M. Berry, "Nonprofits Shouldn't Be Afraid to Lobby," *Chronicle of Philanthropy*, November 27, 2003; Marion R. Fremont Smith, *Governing Nonprofit Organizations: Federal and State Law and Regulations* (Cambridge, MA: Harvard University Press, 2004); John Simon, Harvey Dale, and Laura Chisolm, "Federal Tax Treatment of Charitable Organizations," in *The Nonprofit Sector: A Research Handbook*, 1st ed., ed. Walter W. Powell and Richard Steinberg (New Haven, CT: Yale University Press, 2006), 267–306.

33. John Edie, "A Lift for Lobbying," *Foundation News* 32, no. 2 (1991): 40–45; Brent S. Andersen, "Foundations as Political Actors: Their Efforts to Shape Interest Group Movements, the Policy-Making Process, and Public Policy Outcomes" (Unpublished dissertation, Madison, WI: University of Wisconsin–Madison, 2002); Lucy Bernholz, Stephanie Linden Seale, and Tony Wang, "Building to Last: Field Building as Philanthropic Strategy," Blueprint Research and Design (2010), http://www.arabellaadvisors.com/wp-content/uploads/2012/03/building-to-last.pdf.

34. Bartley (2007) analyzes how foundations were central in building a new field of international forest certification, involving both corporate and governmental actors in the process. Bartley illuminates how several large foundations convened organizations from multiple sectors to create a centralized, independent authorizing body to certify sustainably harvested wood on an international market. This case of foundation-sponsored field building provides an example of a policy-related initiative that was not explicitly governed under the auspices of the state.

Instead, it resides primarily in the nonprofit sector and involves partnerships across a distributed group of organizations, and thus avoids scrutiny with regard to the appropriateness of foundation actions.

35. Following the fallout of the Tax Reform Act, consensus emerged in the foundation field that unlike up-front activism, implementation after the fact was a safe area of investment for foundation resources in policy. Accordingly, foundations have a history of assisting with policy reform implementation following major legislative victories at multiple levels of government. McKersie (1998) analyzes how eleven Chicago foundations were involved in the policy environment surrounding the passage of the 1988 Chicago School Reform Act. The implementation of the governance reforms in the seven-year period following the legislation, which mandated school district recentralization after an era of local school self-governance, was described as "the most radical state legislative act of the century regarding urban education" (xv). Instead of attempting to initiate these governance reforms, these foundations chose to focus on their implementation following the legislation's passage. The foundations were not strategically involved in the development of the act from its inception but instead responded reactively as "enablers." During the five years after the legislation's passage, they contributed 90 percent of the total $26 million contributed to the effort (8). McKersie indicates that this helped to sustain the issue on the state's policy agenda for a decade after the passage of the act, in contrast to more common "seed and leave" strategies—or foundations' more common strategy of piloting social-sector programs and then turning their implementation over to the state. Instead, the Chicago foundations engaged with the policy process on a more extensive and long-term scale. They built coalitions both with government actors and with carefully maintained networks of grassroots actors, mandating extensive community building and partnership with parent and community involvement in school reform governance.

36. Despite the statute's strict provisions, the final Tax Reform Act was actually much less severe than some proposals that Congress had weighed. In 1964, Senator Albert Gore Sr. had introduced a measure that would end the charitable deductibility of donations to private foundations. In 1969, the Senate Finance Committee had considered a proposal to prohibit all foundations from engaging in any form of activity "intended to influence the decision of any governmental body." These proposals were not included in the eventual legislation, in large part due to the Rockefeller family's ties to government officials and their efforts to organize a nonpartisan group, the Peterson Commission, that issued recommendations about appropriate regulations on foundations. The Peterson Commission represented a coordinated attempt by foundations to proactively minimize the potentially harmful implications of the Tax Reform Act.

37. Waldemar A. Nielsen, *The Big Foundations* (New York, NY: Columbia University Press, 1972); Karl and Katz, "The American Private Philanthropic Foundation and the Public Sphere 1890–1930," 236–270; J. Craig Jenkins, "Channeling Social

Protest: Foundation Patronage of Contemporary Social Movements," in *Private Action and the Public Good*, ed. Walter W. Powell and Elisabeth S. Clemens (New Haven, CT: Yale University Press, 1998), 206–216; J. Craig Jenkins and Abigail Halcli, "Grassrooting the System? The Development and Impact of Social Movement Philanthropy, 1953–1990," in *Philanthropic Foundations, New Scholarship, New Possibilities*, ed. Ellen Condliffe Lagemann (Bloomington, IN: Indiana University Press, 1999), 229–256; Peter Frumkin, "The Long Recoil from Regulation: Private Philanthropic Foundations and the Tax Reform Act of 1969," *The American Review of Public Administration* 28, no. 3 (1998): 266–286; Peter Frumkin, "Trouble in Foundationland: Looking Back, Looking Ahead," (2004); Susan A. Ostrander, "Legacy and Promise for Social Justice Funding: Charitable Foundations and Progressive Social Movements, Past and Present," in *Foundations for Social Change: Critical Perspectives on Philanthropy and Popular Movements*, ed. Daniel Faber and Deborah McCarthy (Lanham, MD: Rowman & Littlefield, 2005), 33–60.

38. Scholars have agreed that foundations have been largely reticent to support grassroots political change, community organizing, and political advocacy by social movement organizations, despite some historically celebrated funding of the civil rights movement. Instead, a small but well-developed body of work has shown that foundations tend to opt for less politically tenuous means of influencing the policy process. In the 1960s, some foundations began to show interest in funding efforts for broad-based social change, such as the civil rights and women's movements (Jenkins and Halcli, 1999; Faber and McCarthy, 2005). However, research by the Donee Group, which was created to inform the Committee on Private Philanthropy and Public Need (later the Filer Commission), found that funding targeted toward social movements or social justice was limited. Jenkins and Eckert (1986) substantiate this claim in their examination of elite patronage of the civil rights movement and related "black insurgency." Rather than driving and instigating social change in the civil rights movement, foundation support actually lagged key periods of movement activity, indicating that foundations were indeed primarily reactive rather than proactive in their sponsorship of social change. In addition, Jenkins (1983) found that foundation support actually changed the movement from originator goals to more moderate objectives. Several accounts concur that while social movement philanthropy became more popular between the 1970s and 1990s, on the whole, foundations were cautious about the ramifications of appearing radical for their social legitimacy and were concerned about tax exemption for engaging in ostensibly political activity through funding grassroots political movements (Nagai, Lerner, and Rothman, 1994; Bothwell, 2005; Ostrander, 2006). As Bothwell (2005, 119) stated, "Very limited philanthropic funding of social activism and nonprofit advocacy" remained the norm during this period. Haines (1988, 114) noted that following the Tax Reform Act, the thirty-three largest foundations (with assets of $100

million or more) were more "on the trailing edge than the cutting edge of change."

39. Jenkins's studies are part of a broader spectrum of literature on foundation support to social movements. This tradition generally finds that foundations' involvement diverts movements from the realm of contentious grassroots politics to professional, moderate goals. At one end, "channeling" theory argues that foundations "cherry-pick" moderate organizations within social movements, privileging professionalized organizations and diverting movements from their original grassroots-oriented goals, such as protest (Jenkins and Eckert, 1986; Jenkins, 1998; Jenkins and Halcli, 1999). Toward the middle of the spectrum, "co-optation" theorists argue that foundations fund moderate social change organizations rather than radical ones that might challenge entrenched interests, also reflecting a bias toward a conservative status quo (Jenkins, 1998). At the most critical end, "corporatism" theorists posit that philanthropic foundations perpetuate established interests, and their support for social change advocacy is designed to maintain systemic social control of the ruling class, thus resulting in anathema for social movements (Piven and Cloward, 1977; Roelofs, 2003). Thus, the literature on foundations' influence in social movements is, in summary, skeptical: philanthropic elites professionalize social movement organizations and lag support behind key social movement events, as opposed to initiating or facilitating social change efforts (Jenkins, 1983); or introduce oligarchy and institutionalization that thwart originator goals (Piven and Cloward, 1977). With a few exceptions (McCarthy and Zald, 1977), scholars agree with Jenkins's findings that foundation funding tends to professionalize social movement organizations and that foundations lag support behind key social movement events, as opposed to initiating social change efforts (Jenkins 1983).

40. John G. Simon, "Foundations and Public Controversy: An Affirmative View," in *The Future of Foundations*, ed. Fritz F. Heimann (Saddle River, NJ: Prentice Hall, 1973), 58–100.

41. Ellen Condliffe Lagemann, *Private Power for the Public Good: A History of the Carnegie Foundation for the Advancement of Teaching* (Middletown, CT: Wesleyan University Press, 1983), 53.

42. Robert A. Kronley and Claire Handley, *Maturing Investments: Philanthropy and Middle Grades Reform*, (2003); James M. Ferris and Michael Mintrom, *Foundations and Public Policymaking: A Conceptual Framework* (Los Angeles, CA: Center on Philanthropy and Public Policy, University of Southern California, 2002).

43. Carr, "Private Voices, Public Forces: Agenda Setting and the Power of Foundations in the NCLB Era." Unpublished dissertation.

44. Scott, "The Politics of Venture Philanthropy in Charter School Policy and Advocacy," 106–108.

CHAPTER 2

Anderson, Eric, and Alfred A. Moss Jr. *Dangerous Donations: Northern Philanthropy and Southern Black Education, 1902–1930*. Columbia, MO: University of Missouri Press, 1999.

Anderson, James D. *The Education of Blacks in the South, 1860–1935*. Chapel Hill, NC: University of North Carolina Press, 1988.

Bacchetti, Ray, and Thomas Ehrlich. *Reconnecting Education and Foundations*. San Francisco, CA: Jossey-Bass, 2007.

Barkan, Joanne. "Got Dough? How Billionaires Rule Our Schools." *Dissent*, Winter 2011. https://www.dissentmagazine.org/artcle/got-dough-how-billionaires-rule-our-schools.

Carr, Patrick Joseph. "Private Voices, Public Forces: Agenda Setting and the Power of Foundations in the NCLB Era." Unpublished dissertation. Washington, DC: Georgetown University, 2011.

Confessore, Nicholas. "Policy-Making Billionaires." *New York Times*, November 26, 2011.

Greene, Jay, and William C. Symonds. "Bill Gates Gets Schooled." *Bloomberg Businessweek*, June 25, 2006.

Hess, Frederick M. *With the Best of Intentions: How Philanthropy Is Reshaping K–12 Education*. Cambridge, MA: Harvard Education Press, 2005.

Johnson, Victoria. "What Is Organizational Imprinting? Cultural Entrepreneurship in the Founding of the Paris Opera." *American Journal of Sociology* 113, no. 1, (2007): 97–127.

Kohl-Arenas, Erica. "Can Philanthropy Ever Reduce Inequality?" *Open Democracy*, July 8, 2015. https://www.opendemocracy.net/transformation/erica-kohlarenas/can-philanthropy-ever-reduce-inequality.

Otterman, Sharon. "New York City Abandons Teacher Bonus Program." *New York Times*, July 17, 2011.

Reckhow, Sarah. *Follow the Money: How Foundation Dollars Change Public School Politics*. New York, NY: Oxford University Press, 2013.

Scott, Janelle. "The Politics of Venture Philanthropy in Charter School Policy and Advocacy." *Educational Policy* 23, no. 1 (2009): 106–136.

Smith, James Allen. *Foundations and Public Policymaking: A Historical Perspective*. Los Angeles, CA: Center on Philanthropy and Public Policy, University of Southern California, 2002.

Snyder, Jeffrey W. "How Old Foundations Differ from New Foundations." In *The New Education Philanthropy: Politics, Policy, and Reform*, edited by Frederick M. Hess and Jeffrey Henig, 29–54. Cambridge, MA: Harvard Education Press, 2015.

Stanfield, John. *Philanthropy and Jim Crow in American Social Science*. Westport, CT: Greenwood Press, 1985.

Stinchcombe, Arthur. "Social Structure and Organizations." In *Handbook of Organizations*, edited by James March, 142–193. New York, NY: Rand McNally, 1965.

1. Nicholas Confessore, "Policy-Making Billionaires," *New York Times*, November 26, 2011.

2. John Stanfield, *Philanthropy and Jim Crow in American Social Science* (Westport, CT: Greenwood Press, 1985); James D. Anderson, *The Education of Blacks in the South, 1860–1935* (Chapel Hill, NC: University of North Carolina Press, 1988); Eric Anderson and Alfred A. Moss Jr., *Dangerous Donations: Northern Philanthropy and Southern Black Education, 1902–1930* (Columbia, MO: University of Missouri Press, 1999).

3. Many of the demonstration projects cited in the literature are interesting both for their significant impact on state programs as well as their unintended involvement in racial politics. The earliest examples of demonstration projects occurred in the Reconstruction era in the South, when Northern philanthropists began to invest in universal education for white children and incorporated the involvement of the state to achieve greater scale for these initiatives. Smith (2002) recounts that as early as 1867, the Peabody Fund leveraged its governing board in order to garner public support for its goal. A successor to the Peabody Fund, the Rosenwald Fund partnered with local and state governments to leverage nearly $18 million in tax revenue toward building primary schools for black children and homes for black teachers between 1917 and 1932 and later supported the establishment of normal schools that laid the foundation for historically black colleges and universities (Anderson, 1988; Anderson and Moss, 1999; Smith, 2002; Scott, 2009). Rosenwald also supported vocational and industrial training programs, such as the Tuskegee Institute. Among other mechanisms, the Rosenwald Fund "built human capital through teacher and library training programs and a vast national fellowship program [and] it deployed some of that human capital in local and state government agencies, paying salaries for a fixed period until governments were ready to pick up the costs" (Smith, 2002). Similar to the Carnegie's funding of social science work on race, however, Rosenwald represented a paternalistic orientation in its pursuit of creating opportunities for black citizens. As Scott notes (2009, 111): "Although there is no question that these institutions provided opportunities for students that otherwise might not have existed, the schools were also originally organized around specific notions of what African Americans' social status should be, usually aligned with training students for industrial and service work."

4. Ray Bacchetti and Thomas Ehrlich, *Reconnecting Education and Foundations: Turning Good Intentions into Educational Capital* (San Francisco, CA: Jossey-Bass, 2007).

5. Frederick M. Hess, *With the Best of Intentions: How Philanthropy Is Reshaping K–12 Education* (Cambridge, MA: Harvard Education Press, 2005).

6. Janelle Scott, "The Politics of Venture Philanthropy in Charter School Policy and Advocacy," *Educational Policy* 23, no. 1 (2009): 106–136; Sarah Reckhow, *Follow the Money: How Foundation Dollars Change Public School Politics* (New York, NY: Oxford University Press, 2013); Jeffrey W. Snyder, "How Old Foundations

Differ From New Foundations," in *The New Education Philanthropy*, ed. Frederick M. Hess and Jeffrey Henig (Cambridge, MA: Harvard Education Press, 2015), 29–54.

7. Jay Greene and William C. Symonds, "Bill Gates Gets Schooled," *Bloomberg Businessweek*, June 25, 2006.

8. Joanne Barkan, "Got Dough? How Billionaires Rule Our Schools," *Dissent*, Winter 2011, https://www.dissentmagazine.org/article/got-dough-how-billionaires-rule-our-schools.

9. Sharon Otterman, "New York City Abandons Teacher Bonus Program," *New York Times*, July 17, 2011.

10. Arthur Stinchcombe, "Social Structure and Organizations." In *Handbook of Organizations*, ed. James March (New York, NY: Rand McNally, 1965), 142–193; Victoria Johnson, "What Is Organizational Imprinting? Cultural Entrepreneurship in the Founding of the Paris Opera," *American Journal of Sociology* 113, no. 1 (2007): 97–127.

11. Erica Kohl-Arenas, "Can Philanthropy Ever Reduce Inequality?", *Open Democracy*, July 8, 2015, https://www.opendemocracy.net/transformation/erica-kohlarenas/can-philanthropy-ever-reduce-inequality.

CHAPTER 3

Brest, Paul. "A Decade of Outcome-Oriented Philanthropy." *Stanford Social Innovation Review* 10, no. 2 (2012): 42–47.

Brest, Paul, and Hal Harvey. *Money Well Spent: A Strategic Plan for Smart Philanthropy*. New York, NY: Bloomberg Press, 2008.

DiMaggio, Paul. "Constructing an organizational field as a professional project." In *The New Institutionalism in Organizational Analysis*, edited by Walter Powell and Paul DiMaggio, 267–292. Chicago, IL: University of Chicago Press, 1991.

Frumkin, Peter. "Inside Venture Philanthropy." *Society* 40 (2003): 7–15.

———. *Strategic Giving: The Art and Science of Philanthropy*. Chicago, IL: University of Chicago Press, 2006.

Fulton, Katherine, and Andrew Blau. *Looking Out for the Future: An Orientation for 21st Century Philanthropists*. New York, NY: Global Business Institute and the Monitor Institute, 2005.

Greene, Jay P. "Buckets into the Sea: Why Philanthropy Isn't Changing Schools, and How It Could." In *With the Best of Intentions: How Philanthropy Is Reshaping K–12 Education*, edited by Frederick M. Hess, 49–76. Cambridge, MA: Harvard Education Press, 2005.

Gronbjerg, Kirsten, and Lester M. Salamon. "Devolution, Marketization, and the Changing Shape of Government-Nonprofit Relations." In *The State of Nonprofit America*, edited by Lester M. Salamon, 447–470. Washington, DC: Brookings Institution Press, 2003.

Habermas, Jürgen. *Toward a Rational Society: Student Protest, Science, and Politics*. Boston, MA: Beacon Press, 1970.

Hood, Christopher. "A Public Management for All Seasons?" *Public Administration* 69, no. 1 (1991): 3–19.

Hwang, Hokyu, and Walter W. Powell. "The Rationalization of Charity: The Influences of Professionalism in the Nonprofit Sector." *Administrative Science Quarterly* 54, no. 2 (2009): 268–298.

Kettl, Donald F. *The Global Public Management Revolution*. Washington, DC: Brookings Institution Press, 2005.

Khurana, Rakesh. *From Higher Aims to Hired Hands: The Social Transformation of American Business Schools and the Unfulfilled Promise of Management as a Profession*. Princeton, NJ: Princeton University Press, 2007.

Lagemann, Ellen Condliffe. *The Politics of Knowledge: The Carnegie Corporation, Philanthropy, and Public Policy*. Chicago, IL: University of Chicago Press, 1989.

Letts, Christine W., William Ryan, and Allen Grossman. "Virtuous Capital: What Foundations Can Learn from Venture Capitalists." *Harvard Business Review* 75, no. 2 (1997): 36–44.

Morozov, Evgeny. "Don't Be Evil." *New Republic*, July 13, 2011.

Parker, Sean. "Philanthropy for Hackers." *Wall Street Journal*, June 26, 2015.

Quinn, Rand, Megan Tompkins-Stange, and Debra Meyerson. "Beyond Grantmaking: Philanthropic Foundations as Agents of Change and Institutional Entrepreneurs." *Nonprofit and Voluntary Sector Quarterly* 43, no. 6 (2014): 950–968.

Radin, Beryl A. *Challenging the Performance Movement: Accountability, Complexity, and Democratic Values*. Washington, DC: Georgetown University Press, 2006.

Reckhow, Sarah. *Follow the Money: How Foundation Dollars Change Public School Politics*. New York, NY: Oxford University Press, 2013.

Scott, Janelle. "The Politics of Venture Philanthropy in Charter School Policy and Advocacy." *Educational Policy* 23, no. 1 (2009): 106–136.

Seidenstat, Paul. "Theory and Practice of Contracting Out in the United States." In *Contracting Out Government Services*, edited by Paul Seidenstat, 3–25. Westport, CT: Praeger, 1999.

Sievers, Bruce R. "If Pigs Had Wings: The Appeals and Limits of Venture Philanthropy." *Foundation News and Commentary* 38, no. 6 (2004): 44–46.

———. "Philanthropy's Role in Liberal Democracy." *Journal of Speculative Philosophy* 24, no. 4 (2010): 380–398.

Snyder, Jeffrey W. "How Old Foundations Differ from New Foundations." In *The New Education Philanthropy: Politics, Policy, and Reform*, edited by Frederick M. Hess and Jeffrey Henig, 29–54. Cambridge, MA: Harvard Education Press, 2015.

Suarez, David. "Street Credentials and Management Backgrounds: Careers of Nonprofit Executives in an Evolving Sector." *Nonprofit and Voluntary Sector Quarterly* 39, no. 4 (2009): 696–716.

Townley, Barbara, David J. Cooper, and Leslie Oakes. "Performance Measures and the Rationalization of Organizations." *Organization Studies* 24, no. 7 (2003): 1045–1071.

1. "Field-building" has long been a preferred philanthropic strategy across many fields, particularly in terms of professionalization of existing fields. For example, the Carnegie Corporation was a major player in the art museum field during the early decades of the twentieth century, funding national professional associations and underwriting the professional development of museum staffers, resulting in the rise of a populist museum education model and the demise of a traditional connoisseurship model (DiMaggio, 1991). Similarly, Carnegie and Ford were central in transforming the field of management education in the 1980s and 1990s by funding doctoral fellowships, sponsoring conferences for business school leaders, and supporting faculty research, conferring legitimacy and elite status on those business schools that met high standards (Khurana, 2007).

2. See, for example, Peter Frumkin, *Strategic Giving: The Art and Science of Philanthropy* (Chicago, IL: University of Chicago Press, 2006); Paul Brest and Hal Harvey, *Money Well Spent: A Strategic Plan for Smart Philanthropy* (New York, NY: Bloomberg Press, 2008); Paul Brest, "A Decade of Outcome-Oriented Philanthropy," *Stanford Social Innovation Review* 10, no. 2 (2012): 42–47; Janelle Scott, "The Politics of Venture Philanthropy in Charter School Policy and Advocacy," *Educational Policy* 23, no. 1 (2009): 106–136; Sarah Reckhow, *Follow the Money: How Foundation Dollars Change Public School Politics* (New York, NY: Oxford University Press, 2013).

3. "Venture philanthropy" is a concept often interchanged with "strategic philanthropy," and was popularized by a 1997 *Harvard Business Review* article by Letts, Grossman, and Ryan. Like strategic philanthropy, venture philanthropy is results-driven but derives specific components of its operations directly from a venture capital model. The term *venture philanthropy* was popularized in the late 1990s. Venture philanthropy applies the principles of venture capital funding to the social sector. It emphasizes seeking out grantees rather than issuing open calls for proposals, conducting extensive due diligence on potential grantees prior to investments so as to ensure aggressive return on investment, high engagement with grantees and provision of management assistance, including assuming board seats; close monitoring and quantifiable measurement of results; and exit strategies (Letts, Ryan and Grossman, 1997; Frumkin, 2003; Sievers, 2004). Venture philanthropies are explicit in their desire for scaling promising new innovations to achieve catalytic impact beyond local contexts.

4. Scott, "The Politics of Venture Philanthropy in Charter School Policy and Advocacy," 106–136; Jeffrey W. Snyder, "How Old Foundations Differ from New Foundations," in *The New Education Philanthropy*, ed. Frederick M. Hess and Jeffrey Henig (Cambridge, MA: Harvard Education Press, 2015), 29–54.

5. Bruce R. Sievers, "Philanthropy's Role in Liberal Democracy," *Journal of Speculative Philosophy* 24, no. 4 (2010): 380–398.

6. Ibid.

7. Scott, "The Politics of Venture Philanthropy in Charter School Policy and Advocacy," 106–136; Rand Quinn, Megan Tompkins-Stange, and Debra Meyerson,

"Beyond Grantmaking: Philanthropic Foundations as Agents of Change and Institutional Entrepreneurs," *Nonprofit and Voluntary Sector Quarterly* 43, no. 6 (2014): 950–968.

8. Quinn et al., "Beyond Grantmaking: Philanthropic Foundations as Agents of Change and Institutional Entrepreneurs," 950–968.

9. Ibid.

10. Snyder, "How Old Foundations Differ from New Foundations," 29–54.

11. Scott, "The Politics of Venture Philanthropy in Charter School Policy and Advocacy," 106–136.

12. Katherine Fulton and Andrew Blau, *Looking Out for the Future: An Orientation for 21st Century Philanthropists* (New York, NY: Global Business Institute and the Monitor Institute, 2005).

13. Jay P. Greene, "Buckets into the Sea: Why Philanthropy Isn't Changing Schools, and How It Could," in *With the Best of Intentions: How Philanthropy Is Reshaping K–12 Education*, ed. Frederick M. Hess, (Cambridge, MA: Harvard Education Press, 2005), 49–76.

14. See, for example, Christopher Hood, "A Public Management for All Seasons?", *Public Administration* 69, no. 1 (1991): 3–19; Paul Seidenstat, "Theory and Practice of Contracting Out in the United States," in *Contracting Out Government Services*, ed. Paul Seidenstat (Westport, CT: Praeger, 1999), 3–25; Barbara Townley, David J. Cooper, and Leslie Oakes, "Performance Measures and the Rationalization of Organizations," *Organization Studies* 24, no. 7 (2003): 1045–1071; Kirsten Gronbjerg and Lester M. Salamon, "Devolution, Marketization, and the Changing Shape of Government-Nonprofit Relations," in *The State of Nonprofit America*, ed. Lester M. Salamon (Washington, DC: Brookings Institution Press, 2003), 447–470; Donald F. Kettl, *The Global Public Management Revolution* (Washington, DC: Brookings Institution Press, 2005); Beryl A. Radin, *Challenging the Performance Movement: Accountability, Complexity, and Democratic Values* (Washington, DC: Georgetown University Press, 2006).

15. Hokyu Hwang and Walter W. Powell, "The Rationalization of Charity: The Influences of Professionalism in the Nonprofit Sector," *Administrative Science Quarterly* 54, no. 2 (2009): 268–298; David Suarez, "Street Credentials and Management Backgrounds: Careers of Nonprofit Executives in an Evolving Sector," *Nonprofit and Voluntary Sector Quarterly* 39, no. 4 (2009): 696–716.

16. Jürgen Habermas, *Toward a Rational Society: Student Protest, Science, and Politics* (Boston, MA: Beacon Press, 1970).

17. Hwang and Powell, "The Rationalization of Charity: The Influences of Professionalism in the Nonprofit Sector," 268–298.

18. Evgeny Morozov, "Don't Be Evil," *New Republic*, July 13, 2011.

19. Sean Parker, "Philanthropy for Hackers," *Wall Street Journal*, June 26, 2015.

20. Ellen Condliffe Lagemann, *The Politics of Knowledge: The Carnegie Corporation, Philanthropy, and Public Policy*, 1st ed. Chicago, IL: University of Chicago Press, 1989.

CHAPTER 4

Blume, Howard. "Charter Schools Get Boost." *Los Angeles Times*, January 17, 2008.

Dillon, Sam. "Behind Grass-Roots School Advocacy, Bill Gates." *New York Times*, May 21, 2011.

Ferris, James, and Michael Mintrom. *Foundations and Public Policymaking: A Conceptual Framework*. Los Angeles, CA: Center on Philanthropy and Public Policy, University of Southern California, 2002.

Marris, Peter, and Martin Rein. *Dilemmas of Social Reform: Poverty and Community Action in the United States*. Chicago, IL: University of Chicago Press, 1973.

1. This distinction is sometimes characterized as the difference between indirect versus direct methods of asserting influence (Ferris and Mintrom, 2002). An indirect policy approach involves a one-step-removed orientation toward policy influence, wherein foundations attempt to realize goals primarily through funding grantees. Direct approaches, by contrast, involve foundations assuming active roles as policy influencers.
2. Peter Marris and Martin Rein, *Dilemmas of Social Reform: Poverty and Community Action in the United States*. (Chicago, IL: University of Chicago Press, 1973).
3. Sam Dillon, "Behind Grass-Roots School Advocacy, Bill Gates," *New York Times*, May 21, 2011.
4. Howard Blume, "Charter Schools Get Boost," *Los Angeles Times*, January 17, 2008.

CHAPTER 5

Heifetz, Ronald. *Leadership Without Easy Answers*. Cambridge, MA: Harvard University Press, 1994.

Kania, John, and Mark Kramer. "Collective Impact." *Stanford Social Innovation Review* 9, no. 1 (2011): 36–41.

Nocera, Joe. "Gates Puts the Focus on Teaching." *New York Times*, May 21, 2012.

Schorr, Lisbeth B. "Broader Evidence for Bigger Impact." *Stanford Social Innovation Review* 10, no. 4 (2012): 50–55.

1. Ronald Heifetz, *Leadership Without Easy Answers* (Cambridge, MA: Harvard University Press, 1994); John Kania and Mark Kramer, "Collective Impact," *Stanford Social Innovation Review* 9, no. 1 (2011): 36–41.
2. Joe Nocera, "Gates Puts the Focus on Teaching," *New York Times*, May 21, 2012.
3. Lisbeth B. Schorr, "Broader Evidence for Bigger Impact," *Stanford Social Innovation Review* 10, no. 4 (2012): 50–55.

CHAPTER 6

Anderson, Nick. "Gates Foundation Playing Pivotal Role in Changes for Education System." *Washington Post*, July 12, 2010.

Carr, Patrick Joseph. "Private Voices, Public Forces: Agenda Setting and the Power of Foundations in the NCLB Era." Unpublished dissertation. Washington, DC: Georgetown University, 2011.

deMarrais, Kathleen, Arthur M. Horne, Karen E. Watkins, Claire Suggs, Robert A. Kronley, and Kate Shropshire Swett. "Critical Contributions: Philanthropic Investment in Teachers and Teaching." Atlanta, GA: Kronley & Associates, 2011.
Harmon, Lawrence. "Bill Gates' Risky Adventure." *Boston Globe*, April 27, 2010.
Hwang, Hokyu, and Walter W. Powell. "The Rationalization of Charity: The Influences of Professionalism in the Nonprofit Sector." *Administrative Science Quarterly* 54, no. 2 (2009): 268–298.
Reckhow, Sarah. *Follow the Money: How Foundation Dollars Change Public School Politics.* New York, NY: Oxford University Press, 2013.
Tompkins, Megan. *Normative Dimensions of Philanthropic Power: Case Study of the Gates Foundation.* Stanford Political Science Department Teaching Case, 2007.
US Department of Education. "12 Major Foundations Commit $500 Million to Education Innovation in Concert with U.S. Education Department's $650 Million 'Investing In Innovation' Fund." April 29, 2010. http://www.ed.gov/news/press-releases/12-major-foundations-commit-500-milion-education-innovation-concert-us-education-departments-650-million-investing-innovation-fund.

1. Patrick Carr, *Private Voices, Public Forces: Agenda Setting and the Power of Foundations in the NCLB Era* (Unpublished dissertation, Washington, DC: Georgetown University, 2011), 201.
2. Vartan Gregorian, quoted in US Department of Education, "12 Major Foundations Commit $500 Million to Education Innovation in Concert with U.S. Education Department's $650 Million 'Investing In Innovation' Fund." April 29, 2010. http://www.ed.gov/news/press-releases/12-major-foundations-commit-500-million-education-innovation-concert-us-education-departments-650-million-investing-innovation-fund.
3. Sarah Reckhow, *Follow the Money: How Foundation Dollars Change Public School Politics* (New York, NY: Oxford University Press, 2013), 2.
4. Reckhow shows that foundations are more likely to channel grants to districts under the control of a single actor (such as the mayor or governor) rather than an elected school board, and where a network of supportive nonprofit partners also exists in order to implement desired reforms.
5. Kathleen deMarrais, Arthur M. Horne, Karen E. Watkins, Claire Suggs, Robert A. Kronley, and Kate Shropshire Swett. *Critical Contributions: Philanthropic Investment in Teachers and Teaching* (Atlanta, GA: Kronley & Associates, 2011), 48.
6. Lawrence Harmon, "Bill Gates' Risky Adventure," *Boston Globe*, April 27, 2010.
7. Nick Anderson, "Gates Foundation Playing Pivotal Role in Changes for Education System," *Washington Post*, July 12, 2010.
8. Megan Tompkins, *Normative Dimensions of Philanthropic Power: Case Study of the Gates Foundation*, Stanford Political Science Department Teaching Case, 2007.
9. Hokyu Hwang and Walter W. Powell, "The Rationalization of Charity: The

Influences of Professionalism in the Nonprofit Sector," *Administrative Science Quarterly* 54, no. 2 (2009): 268–298.

CHAPTER 7

Arnove, Robert F., ed. *Philanthropy and Cultural Imperialism: The Foundations at Home and Abroad.* 1st ed. Bloomington, IN: Indiana University Press, 1982.

Bloomfield, David. "Come Clean on Small Schools." *Education Week*, January 24, 2006.

Bremner, Robert H. *American Philanthropy.* Chicago, IL: University of Chicago Press, 1988.

Brest, Paul. "Strategic Philanthropy." *Huffington Post*, November 13, 2008.

Brilliant, Eleanor L. *Private Charity and Public Inquiry: A History of the Filer and Peterson Commissions.* Bloomington, IN: Indiana University Press, 2001.

Brody, Evelyn, and John E. Tyler. "Respecting Foundation and Charity Autonomy: How Public Is Private Philanthropy?" *Chicago-Kent Law Review* 85, no. 2 (2010): 571–617.

Buffett, Peter. "The Charitable-Industrial Complex." *New York Times*, July 26, 2013.

Clemens, Elisabeth S. "The Constitution of Citizens: Political Theories of Nonprofit Organizations." In *The Nonprofit Sector: A Research Handbook*, 2nd ed., edited by Walter W. Powell and Richard Steinberg, 207–220. New Haven, CT: Yale University Press, 2006.

Covington, Sally. *Moving a Public Policy Agenda: The Strategic Philanthropy of Conservative Foundations.* Washington, DC: National Committee for Responsive Philanthropy, 1997.

———. "Right Thinking, Big Grants, and Long-Term Strategy: How Conservative Philanthropies and Think Tanks Transform US Public Policy." *Covert Action Quarterly*, 63 (1998): 1–8.

Faber, Daniel, and Deborah McCarthy. *Foundations for Social Change: Critical Perspectives on Philanthropy and Popular Movements.* Lanham, MD: Rowman & Littlefield, 2005.

Fleishman, Joel L. *The Foundation: A Great American Secret.* New York, NY: Public Affairs, 2009.

Frumkin, Peter. "Accountability and Legitimacy in American Foundation Philanthropy." In *The Legitimacy of Philanthropic Foundations*, edited by Kenneth Prewitt, Mattei Dogan, Steven Heydemann, and Stefan Toepler, 99–122. New York, NY: Russell Sage Foundation, 2006.

———. "Private Foundations as Public Institutions: Regulation, Professionalization, and the Redefinition of Organized Philanthropy." In *Philanthropic Foundations: New Scholarship, New Possibilities*, edited by Ellen Condliffe Lagemann, 69–100. Bloomington, IN: Indiana University Press, 1999.

House of Representatives Committee on Ways and Means. *Hearings Before the Committee on Ways and Means, House of Representatives, Ninety-First Congress, First Session on the Subject of Tax Reform, Principal Subject: Tax Exempt Organizations: Foundations and Treasury Report on Foundations.* 91st Cong. (1969).

Karl, Barry D., and Stanley N. Katz, "The American Private Philanthropic Foundation and the Public Sphere 1890–1930." *Minerva* 19, no. 2 (1981): 236–270.

Kohl-Arenas, Erica. "Can Philanthropy Ever Reduce Inequality?" *Open Democracy.* July 8, 2015. https://www.opendemocracy.net/transformation/erica-kohlarenas/can-philanthropy-ever-reduce-inequality.

Lagemann, Ellen Condliffe. *The Politics of Knowledge: The Carnegie Corporation, Philanthropy, and Public Policy.* Chicago, IL: University of Chicago Press, 1989.

Marris, Peter, and Martin Rein, *Dilemmas of Social Reform: Poverty and Community Action in the United States.* 2nd ed. Chicago, IL: University of Chicago Press, 1973.

Nielsen, Waldemar. *The Golden Donors: A New Anatomy of the Great Foundations.* New York, NY: Penguin Group, 1989.

O'Connor, Alice. "The Ford Foundation and Philanthropic Activism in the 1960s," In *Philanthropic Foundations: New Scholarship, New Possibilities*, edited by Ellen Condliffe Lagemann, 169–194. Bloomington, IN: Indiana University Press, 1999.

———. *Poverty Knowledge: Social Science, Social Policy and the Poor in Twentieth-Century U.S. History.* Princeton, NJ: Princeton University Press, 2001.

Odendahl, Teresa. *Charity Begins at Home: Generosity and Self-Interest among the Philanthropic Elite.* New York, NY: Basic Books, 1991.

Prewitt, Kenneth. "American Foundations: What Justifies Their Unique Privileges and Powers." In *The Legitimacy of Philanthropic Foundations*, edited by Kenneth Prewitt, Mattei Dogan, Steven Heydemann, and Stefan Toepler, 27–48. New York, NY: Russell Sage Foundation, 2006.

Reich, Rob. "What Are Foundations For?" *Boston Review.* March 1, 2013. http://www.bostonreview.net/forum/what-are-foundations/policy-advocates.

Roelofs, Joan. *Foundations and Public Policy: The Mask of Pluralism.* Albany, NY: State University of New York Press, 2003.

Rogers, Robin. "Why Philanthro-Policymaking Matters." *Society* 48, no. 5 (2011): 376–381.

Saltman, Kenneth J. *The Gift of Education: Public Education and Venture Philanthropy.* New York: Palgrave Macmillan, 2010.

Scott, Janelle. "The Politics of Venture Philanthropy in Charter School Policy and Advocacy." *Educational Policy* 23, no. 1 (2009): 106–136.

Simon, John G. "Foundations and Public Controversy: An Affirmative View." In *The Future of Foundations*, edited by Fritz F. Heimann, 58–100. Saddle River, NJ: Prentice Hall, 1973.

Steinberg, Richard. "Economic Theories of Nonprofit Organizations." In *The Nonprofit Sector: A Research Handbook*, 2nd ed., edited by Walter W. Powell and Richard Steinberg, 117–139. New Haven, CT: Yale University Press, 2006.

Teles, Steven M. *The Rise of the Conservative Legal Movement: The Battle for Control of the Law.* Princeton, NJ: Princeton University Press, 2008.

Treasury Department. *Report on Private Foundations, Senate Committee on Finance.* Washington, DC: US Government Printing Office, 1965.

1. Rob Reich, "What Are Foundations For?" *Boston Review*, March 1, 2013, http://www.bostonreview.net/forum/what-are-foundations/policy-advocates.
2. Ibid.
3. John G. Simon, "Foundations and Public Controversy: An Affirmative View," in *The Future of Foundations*, ed. Fritz F. Heimann (Saddle River, NJ: Prentice Hall, 1973), 58–100; Daniel Faber and Deborah McCarthy, *Foundations for Social Change: Critical Perspectives on Philanthropy and Popular Movements* (Lanham, MD: Rowman & Littlefield, 2005); Peter Frumkin, "Accountability and Legitimacy in American Foundation Philanthropy," in *The Legitimacy of Philanthropic Foundations*, ed. Kenneth Prewitt, et al. (New York, NY: Russell Sage Foundation, 2006), 99–122; Evelyn Brody and John E. Tyler, "Respecting Foundation and Charity Autonomy: How Public Is Private Philanthropy?", *Chicago-Kent Law Review* 85, no. 2 (2010): 571–617; Kenneth Prewitt, "American Foundations: What Justifies Their Unique Privileges and Powers," in *The Legitimacy of Philanthropic Foundations*, ed. Kenneth Prewitt, et al. (New York, NY: Russell Sage Foundation, 2006), 27–48.
4. Richard Steinberg, "Economic Theories of Nonprofit Organizations," in *The Nonprofit Sector: A Research Handbook*, 2nd ed., ed. Walter W. Powell and Richard Steinberg (New Haven, CT: Yale University Press, 2006), 117–139.
5. Treasury Department, *Report on Private Foundations, Senate Committee on Finance* (Washington, DC: US Government Printing Office, 1965).
6. Simon, "Foundations and Public Controversy," 82–83.
7. House of Representatives Committee on Ways and Means, *Hearings Before the Committee on Ways and Means, House of Representatives, Ninety-First Congress, First Session on the Subject of Tax Reform, Principal Subject: Tax 230 Exempt Organizations: Foundations and Treasury Report on Foundations*, 91st Cong. (1969) (statement of Alan Pifer, President, Carnegie Corporation, p. 124).
8. House of Representatives Committee on Ways and Means, *Hearings Before the Committee on Ways and Means, House of Representatives, Ninety-First Congress, First Session on the Subject of Tax Reform, Principal Subject: Tax Exempt Organizations: Foundations and Treasury Report on Foundations*, 91st Cong. (1969) (statement of Martha Griffiths, Congressperson, p. 383).
9. Robert F. Arnove, ed., *Philanthropy and Cultural Imperialism: The Foundations at Home and Abroad*, 1st ed. (Bloomington, IN: Indiana University Press, 1982); Joan Roelofs, *Foundations and Public Policy: The Mask of Pluralism* (Albany, NY: State University of New York Press, 2003); Teresa Odendahl, *Charity Begins at Home: Generosity and Self-Interest among the Philanthropic Elite* (New York, NY: Basic Books, 1991); Kenneth J. Saltman, *The Gift of Education: Public Education and Venture Philanthropy* (New York, NY: Palgrave Macmillan, 2010).
10. Peter Marris and Martin Rein, *Dilemmas of Social Reform: Poverty and Community Action in the United States* (Chicago, IL: University of Chicago Press, 1973); Alice

O'Connor, "The Ford Foundation and Philanthropic Activism in the 1960s," in *Philanthropic Foundations: New Scholarship, New Possibilities*, ed. Ellen Condliffe Lagemann (Bloomington, IN: Indiana University Press, 1999), 169–194.

11. Alice O'Connor, *Poverty Knowledge: Social Science, Social Policy and the Poor in Twentieth-Century U.S. History* (Princeton, NJ: Princeton University Press, 2001), 131.

12. Alice O'Connor, "The Ford Foundation and Philanthropic Activism in the 1960s," 180.

13. Elisabeth S. Clemens, "The Constitution of Citizens: Political Theories of Non-profit Organizations," in *The Nonprofit Sector: A Research Handbook*, 2nd ed., ed. Walter W. Powell and Richard Steinberg (New Haven, CT: Yale University Press, 2006), 207–220.

14. Eleanor L. Brilliant, *Private Charity and Public Inquiry: A History of the Filer and Peterson Commissions* (Bloomington, IN: Indiana University Press, 2001).

15. Waldemar Nielsen, *The Golden Donors: A New Anatomy of the Great Foundations* (New York, NY: Penguin Group, 1989), 7.

16. A move toward core operating support rather than project-based support is similar to politically conservative foundations' strategies, which a number of scholars have cited as exceptionally effective in generating a networked conservative political apparatus in the past two decades (Covington, 1997; Covington, 1998; Teles, 2008).

17. Peter Frumkin, "Private Foundations as Public Institutions: Regulation, Professionalization, and the Redefinition of Organized Philanthropy," in *Philanthropic Foundations: New Scholarship, New Possibilities*, ed. Ellen Condliffe Lagemann (Bloomington, IN: Indiana University Press, 1999), 69–100; Joel L. Fleishman, *The Foundation: A Great American Secret* (New York: Public Affairs, 2009).

18. Another recurrent critique of foundations addresses them as the beneficiaries of tax advantages and argues that they must be democratically accountable to the public whose taxes they benefit from. This argument is generally disavowed by scholars but has consistently arisen in public discourse in the past four decades; this may be a result of foundations' efforts to recover from the sanctions placed on them after the Tax Reform Act, as Frumkin (2006) writes: "In an effort to defend philanthropy from further government investigation and regulation, foundations strategically recast themselves as public trusts to be governed by public purposes" (70). Brody and Tyler (2010) elaborate, "Underlying much of these debates is the premise—stated or merely presumed—that foundation and charity assets are 'public money' and that such entities therefore are subject to various public mandates or standards about their missions, operations, and decision-making" (572).

19. In the 1969 Tax Reform Act hearings, Congressman John Byrnes addressed this issue in the following exchange with Ford Foundation president McGeorge Bundy:

 Mr. Byrnes. I think it is appropriate that we look and see what would have happened to these funds if they had not been given to a tax-exempt foundation and had not been eligible for exemption from the estate tax . . . if it had not been for the tax situation, 77 percent of these moneys would really have gone to our public funds. We are then left with a situation, Mr. Bundy, where the judgment of a handful of people determines the use of what might otherwise be public funds. That, it seems to me is where there arises a public responsibility, as opposed to merely the private concern of donors (362).

20. House of Representatives Committee on Ways and Means. Hearings Before the Committee on Ways and Means, House of Representatives, Ninety-First Congress, First Session on the Subject of Tax Reform, Principal Subject: Tax Exempt Organizations: Foundations and Treasury Report on Foundations. 91st Cong. (1969) (statement of Lawrence Stone, Dean of the UC Berkeley School of Law, 167).

21. Paul Brest, "Strategic Philanthropy," *Huffington Post*, November 13, 2008.

22. Barry D. Karl and Stanley N. Katz, "The American Private Philanthropic Foundation and the Public Sphere 1890–1930," *Minerva* 19, no. 2 (1981): 236–270.

23. Ellen Condliffe Lagemann, *The Politics of Knowledge: The Carnegie Corporation, Philanthropy, and Public Policy,* 1st ed. (Chicago, IL: University of Chicago Press, 1989).

24. These observations are underscored by McGeorge Bundy's testimony during the 1969 Tax Reform Act hearings, which argued that private entities were typically proud of the "impressive" endorsement of foundations, rather than being coerced into accepting foundations' resources:

[Public authorities] . . . are generally proud to say that this good idea of their municipality or of their school board of whatever authority may be involved has been so impressive to this outside group that they have a foundation grant for it (420).

25. David Bloomfield, "Come Clean on Small Schools," *Education Week*, January 24, 2006.

26. Janelle Scott, "The Politics of Venture Philanthropy in Charter School Policy and Advocacy," *Educational Policy* 23, no. 1 (2009): 106–136.

A NOTE ABOUT METHODOLOGY

Eisenhardt, K. M. "Building Theories from Case Study Research." *Academy of Management Review* 14, no. 4 (1989): 532–550.

Merriam, Sharan B. *Qualitative Research: A Guide to Design and Implementation,* San Francisco, CA: Jossey-Bass, 2009.

Weiss, Robert Stuart. *Learning from Strangers: The Art and Method of Qualitative Interview Studies.* New York, NY: The Free Press, 1995.

Yin, Robert K. *Case Study Research: Design and Methods.* Thousand Oaks, CA: Sage Publications, 2002.

1. K. M. Eisenhardt, "Building Theories from Case Study Research," *Academy of Management Review* 14, no. 4 (1989): 532–550.

2. Ibid.; Sharan B. Merriam, *Qualitative Research: A Guide to Design and Implementation* (San Francisco: Jossey-Bass, 2009).

3. Robert K. Yin, *Case Study Research: Design and Methods* (Thousand Oaks, CA: Sage Publications, 2002).

4. Robert Stuart Weiss, *Learning from Strangers: The Art and Method of Qualitative Interview Studies* (New York: The Free Press, 1995).

ACKNOWLEDGMENTS

As the story goes, John Steinbeck's friend, Pascal Covici, once found Steinbeck whittling a piece of wood, and said "Why don't you make something for me?" In the dedication to *East of Eden*, Steinberg responded to that request:

> *Well, here's your box. Nearly everything I have is in it . . . the pleasure of design and some despair and the indescribable joy of creation. And on top of all of these are all the gratitude and love I have for you. And still the box is not full.*

At the risk of implying any remote parallel between *East of Eden* and this book, I could not imagine a more fitting way to describe my feelings about this process.

My editor Caroline Chauncey and her team at Harvard Education Press have been a dream to work with, and I am grateful to Frederick Hess for including this book in his series at HEP. I am thankful to the wonderful Stanford faculty who helped shape the book, especially my dissertation advisors, Rob Reich, Woody Powell, Bruce Sievers, and Francisco Ramirez; to Debra Meyerson; and to the Stanford Center on Philanthropy and Civil Society for the institutional and financial support I received as a graduate student. I am deeply appreciative of my community of colleagues at the University of Michigan, and to the faculty, staff, and students at the Ford School, who have been so supportive of my work over the years. Bob Schwartz and Richard Chait, my mentors at the Harvard Graduate School of Education, had a significant impact on my professional trajectory, and I am exceptionally thankful for their belief in me. Many scholar friends have traveled this road with me, and I owe a great debt to Sarah Reckhow, Patricia Bromley, Marisa Bueno, Allison Atteberry, Rand Quinn, Seneca Rosenberg, and Kristine Schutz, among others, all of whom were incredible companions on this journey. I have benefited immeasurably from formative conversations with brilliant colleagues, too numerous to name here, through institutions including SCANCOR's PhD Institute, the Association for Research on Nonprofit Organizations and Voluntary Action, the Philanthropy Lab, the Academy of Management's Public and Nonprofit Division, the Rockefeller Archive Center, and many more, who have influenced my work and challenged my thinking.

Words cannot express my gratitude to my children's teachers, who provided me with complete peace of mind regarding my daughters' care. I give my deepest thanks to my inner circle of beloved friends and to my families, the Winslow-Tompkins and Stanges, who have been great champions and cheerleaders for years. Finally, this book is dedicated to my wonderful parents, who instilled my interests in education and democracy; to my beloved husband and true partner, Kevin; and our daughters, Cora and Lida, who fill my whole heart beyond measure.

And still the box is not full.

ABOUT THE AUTHOR

Megan E. Tompkins-Stange is an Assistant Professor at the Gerald R. Ford School of Public Policy, University of Michigan. She received her PhD from Stanford University in Education Policy and Organization Studies. Her work has been published in *Nonprofit and Voluntary Sector Quarterly*, the *Harvard Journal of Law and Gender*, and in *The New Education Philanthropy: Politics, Policy and Reform*.

INDEX

adaptive problems
  field-oriented approach and, 96
  Kellogg and Ford's viewpoint, 99–101
  technical problems versus, 95–96
Annenberg, Walter, 18
Annenberg Challenge, 18

Berkshire Hathaway, 20
Bill and Melinda Gates Foundation. *See* Gates Foundation
Broad, Eli, 28, 63–64, 77, 84
Broad Center for the Management of School Systems, 29
Broad Foundation
  brand and political capital use, 76–77
  comfort level with policy activism, 19, 43–44
  Common Core involvement, 31–32
  development of leadership pipelines, 29–30
  expectation of proof of impact, 102, 103, 106–108
  federal level activities, 83–84
  founder's influence, 64–65, 77
  founding and endowment, 19, 28
  framing of problems, 95
  grantee management approach, 69–73
  grant-making goal, 28
  illustration of its approach to policy influence, 45
  investment in structural change, 30
  market-based reforms emphasis, 29
  New Orleans school system and, 31
  outcome-oriented approach, 54–55
  partners selection, 80–85
  pay for performance initiatives, 30–31
  quantifiable results focus, 101, 107–108
  redirection of measurement approaches, 106–107
  shift to achieving deeper engagement, 107
  strategy for advancing desired policy targets, 114
  support for CMOs, 57
  technical problems focus, 97, 99–100
  use of leverage, 59–60
  view of its role as a policy actor, 32, 43–45, 59–60, 76–77, 100–101
Broad Residency, 29, 31, 84
Broad Superintendents Academy, 29–30
Buffett, Warren, 7, 20, 59

charter management organizations (CMOs)
  strategic philanthropy concept and, 57
  success in New Orleans, 31
Commission on Industrial Relations, 12
Common Core, 113
  Broad Foundation support, 31–32
  Gates Foundation support, 24, 26, 81
Council of Chief State School Officers, 25, 81
Council on Foundations (COF), 146

Dell Foundation, 57
demonstration projects, 11, 91
Department of Education, US, 81–83,
    113–114
discovery rationale for foundations,
    128–129
Duncan, Arne, 81, 114

Economic Opportunity Act (1964), 12
Education Pioneers, 30
Eli and Edythe Broad Foundation. *See*
    Broad Foundation
evaluation of results. *See* framing
    problems and evaluating results

field-oriented approach to philanthropy
    challenges in managing an intentional
        movement, 4–5
    complexities inherent in, 134
    core questions, 68
    described, 55–56
    grantee management and, 70
    institutional norms involved in, 54–55
    Kellogg and Ford and, 56
    partner selection and, 80
    quantifiable versus integrated results
        and, 102
    technical versus adaptive problems, 96
    traditional philanthropy concept, 57
    worldview of, 127–128
Ford Foundation
    adaptive problems focus, 99–101
    argument for policy advocacy, 60–61
    brand and political capital use, 79
    combination of strategies approach,
        89–90

comfort level with visible policy
    activism, 19
desire for integrated results, 101–102
education program's focus, 39
field-oriented approach, 56
founding and endowment, 19–20, 37
framing of problems, 95
grantee management, 69–70, 73–74, 93
Gray Areas program, 11–12, 50, 133–134
"insider" strategies, 91–94
measuring results approach, 110–111
mission and goals, 37
"outsider" strategies, 90–91, 93–94
partners selection, 89–94
preference for safe strategies, 51
professional culture of, 65–66
reorganization around systemic
    inequality, 39–40, 148
school finance reform goal, 38
social justice commitment, 38–39
view of any foundation's ability to
    directly create change, 108
view of its role as a policy actor, 19, 40,
    49–51, 59, 75, 100
view of leverage, 60, 61, 62–63
view of quantitative evaluations, 109, 110
foundation activism. *See also*
    foundations' philosophies
agenda sustainability amidst
    leadership change, 117–118
argument to delegate control to
    grantees, 133
Broad Foundation's view on, 43–45,
    59–60, 76–77, 100–101
concerns about foundation-endorsed
    reforms, 115–117
consultant mentality in philanthropy,
    121–122

in a democracy (see philanthropy and
    democracy)
effects of mid-course corrections,
    118–120
empirical data's role and value in
    reform initiatives, 122–123
Ford Foundation's view of, 40, 49–51,
    59, 75, 100
foundations' capitalization of federal
    programs, 113–114
foundations' strategy for advancing
    desired policy targets, 114
Gates Foundation's view on, 27, 41–43,
    59, 76–77, 100–101
Kellogg Foundation's view of, 45–49,
    59, 75, 89, 100–101
potential for bias in foundation-
    funded research, 123–125
tensions when outsiders try to impose
    change, 120–121, 125
foundation funding to education
CMOs and, 31, 57
Common Core support, 24, 26, 31–32,
    81, 113
focus of new philanthropists, 18
history of, 18
impact of the Annenberg Challenge, 18
influence of foundation dollars, 17
mandated annual payout requirement, 20
small schools initiative, 21–22, 104–
    105, 119
foundations' philosophies. *See also*
    foundation activism
argument for policy advocacy, 59–61
contrasts in approaches to policy
    work, 53–54, 59
field-oriented approach, 55
at Gates and Broad, 54–55

influence of the founder and, 63–65, 77
institutional norms in engagement,
    54–55
at Kellogg and Ford, 56
leveraging policy as a means versus an
    end, 62–63
main contrasts in approaches, 59
outcome-oriented approach, 54–56,
    67–68
shift in what expertise is most valued,
    66–68
strategic philanthropy concept, 56–58
view of a role as a policy actor, 75
framing problems and evaluating results
adaptive problems focus of Kellogg
    and Ford, 99–101
desire for data in the field of
    philanthropy, 110
differences between the four
    foundations, 95
integrated results approach of Kellogg
    and Ford, 108–112
outcome- versus field-oriented
    approaches, 55
quantifiable results focus of Gates and
    Broad, 102–108
quantifiable versus integrated results,
    101–102
technical problems focus of Gates and
    Broad, 96–99
technical versus adaptive problems,
    95–101, 112

Gates, Bill, 20, 27, 59, 63–64, 77, 97
Gates Foundation
adoption of a state-level-based
    initiative, 24–25

Gates Foundation, *continued*
amount of resources allocated to
advocacy efforts, 27–28
argument for policy advocacy, 59–60
belief in the power of data, 64–65
brand and political capital use, 43, 76–77
Buffett gift's impact, 7, 20–21
comfort level with visible policy
activism, 19
concerns about foundation-endorsed
reforms, 115–117
consideration of grantees' lobbying
activities, 42–43
debut of its grasstops strategy, 81
evolution to engagement in direct
advocacy, 26–27
expectation of proof of impact, 102–
105, 111
focus on systems aligned with policy
changes, 25–26
foundations' responsibility to the
public at large and, 135–136
founder's influence, 64–65, 77
founding and endowment, 19–20
framing of problems, 95
grantee management approach, 69–73
grassroots advocacy and, 82–83
original organization of its grant-
making programs, 20
outcome-oriented approach, 54–55
partners selection, 80–85
potential for bias in foundation-
funded research, 123–125
quantifiable results focus, 101–102
redirection of measurement
approaches, 104, 109, 111
results of education-structure reform
efforts, 21–22
safeguards used to stay within legal
boundaries, 41–42
securing of relationships with elite
federal actors, 81–82
shift to investments in research, 22–23
small schools initiative, 21–22, 104–
105, 119
strategy for advancing desired policy
targets, 114
support for CMOs, 57
technical problems focus, 96–99101
view of its role as a policy actor, 19, 27,
41–43, 59, 76–77, 101
grantee management
argument to delegate control to
grantees, 133
centralized control by Gates and
Broad, 70–73
centralized versus decentralized
approaches, 69–70
consideration of grantees' lobbying
activities at Gates, 42–43
decentralized control by Kellogg and
Ford, 70, 73–76
use of brand and political capital in,
76–77
Gray Areas program, 11–12, 50, 113,
133–134
Greene, Jay, 59–60

hookworm intervention, 11

Independent Sector, 146
integrated results
compared to quantifiable results, 101–
102

field-oriented approach and, 102
Kellogg and Ford and, 108–112
Investing in Innovation (i3) Fund, 25, 113

Kellogg Foundation
adaptive problems focus, 99–101
argument for policy advocacy, 60–61
bottom-up engagement strategy, 85–
86, 88–89
brand and political capital use, 77–79
comfort level with visible policy
activism, 19, 47–48
concern for public opinion, 48–49
desire for integrated results, 101–102
field-oriented approach, 56
founding and endowment, 19, 32
framing of problems, 95
grantee management approach, 69–
70, 73–76
interconnected approach to program
areas, 33–35
mission, 32
partners selection, 85–89
policy agenda development status, 87–
89
primary policy strategy, 75–76
professional culture of, 65–66, 88–89
program areas, 32–33
questioning of methods of
quantitative evaluation, 110
restructuring of the organization, 35
view of any foundation's ability to
directly create change, 108–109
view of its role as a policy actor, 19,
35–37, 45–49, 59, 75, 86–89, 100–
101
view of leverage, 60–62

lobbying and advocacy regulations
congressional action against lobbying
by foundations, 13–14
consideration of grantees' lobbying
activities at Gates, 42–43
foundations' view of federal
restrictions, 141–143

Measures of Effective Teaching project, 22
Microsoft Corporation, 20, 27

National Governors Association, 24, 81
New Leaders for New Schools, 30
New Orleans school system, 31
NewSchools Venture Fund, 57–58, 82
New Standards Project, 98
No Child Left Behind (2001), 22

outcome-oriented approach to
philanthropy
challenges in managing an intentional
movement, 3–4
core questions, 67–68
described, 54–56
dominance of managerial values in, 125
entrepreneurial mindset in, 58
at Gates and Broad, 54–55, 58
grantee management and, 55, 70
growing preference for, 144–145
institutional norms involved in, 54–55
partners selection and, 55, 80
policy initiatives within education
and, 57
quantifiable versus integrated results
and, 102

outcome-oriented approach to
philanthropy, *continued*
strategic philanthropy concept and,
56–58
technical versus adaptive problems,
96
worldview of, 127–128

partners selection
grassroots versus grasstops, 80, 94
strategies of Gates and Broad, 80–85
strategy at Ford, 89–94
strategy at Kellogg, 85–89
value of democratically generated
input and, 94
pay for performance initiatives, 29–31, 57
Pay for Performance Pilot, 30
Peabody Fund, 18
philanthropy and democracy
accountability argument, 140–141
addressing of the underlying
institution of philanthropy, 148–149
board diversity and, 137–138
building nonprofit infrastructure and,
137
challenges of democratic engagement,
134
complexities inherent in field-oriented
strategies, 134
critiques about foundations' responsi-
bilities, 128, 135–136, 143–144
elite networks and the grant-making
process, 136–137
extent of discussion on the work of
foundations, 146–148
foundations' ability to foster
democracy, 129–131

foundations' ability to foster
innovation, 128–129
foundation transparency and, 138–140
lobbying and advocacy regulations
and, 141–143
obligation to act democratically
argument, 145–146
outcome-oriented versus field-
oriented worldviews, 127–128
plutocratic pluralism and, 131–132
preference for the outcome-oriented
approach, 144–145
process through which a worldview
becomes "common sense," 145
questions about the role of foundations
in a liberal democracy, 6
results of the Gray Areas program,
133
tensions about the value of
democratically generated input, 94
philanthropy in the public realm
absence of critical analysis of the
implications of influence, 9
attitude toward foundations'
involvement in policy contexts, 6–7
basis of private foundations' influence
in the public arena, 10–11
challenges in managing an intentional
movement, 3–5
congressional action to prohibit
lobbying by foundations, 13–14
congressional-level concern about
foundations' policy-related
activities, 12–13
critiques of philanthropic involvement
in policy, 7–8
foundations' conceptualization of
policy, 15

foundations' initiation of health and
social programs, 11–12
foundations' institutional opaqueness,
8–9
foundations' success in advancing
goals, 6
foundation staff members' desire for
anonymity, 9–10
market-inspired stance, 57–58
negotiating a role in the public sphere,
5–6
origins of foundations' engagement in
policy contexts, 11
output versus input legitimacy, 7
past reaction to foundations as
political actors, 12
private foundations' asset holdings, 2
recent developments due to, 1–2
Tax Reform Act effects, 13–14
tension between general and project
support, 99–100
view of the use of private wealth to
advance public policy, 10
pluralism rationale for foundations,
129–131
policy activism. *See* foundation activism
Progressive Era, 11, 67

Race to the Top, 25, 82, 113
Reconstruction era, 18
Robertson Foundation, 57
Rockefeller Foundation, 11–12, 59, 136
Rosenwald Fund, 18

small schools initiative by the Gates
Foundation, 21–22, 104–105, 119
strategic philanthropy concept, 56–58,
144–145

Tax Reform Act (1969), 13–14, 50, 115,
130–131, 136, 144, 147
technical problems
adaptive problems versus, 95–96, 99–
101, 112
belief in the power of data at Gates,
64–65
dominance of a desire for data in the
field of philanthropy, 110
empirical data's role and value in
reform initiatives, 122–123
field-oriented approach and, 96
of Gates and Broad, 96–99
traditional philanthropy concept, 57–58

quantifiable results. *See also* technical
problems
compared to integrated results, 101–102
field-oriented approach and, 102
Gates's and Broad's preference for,
102–108

Walsh Commission, 12
W. K. Kellogg Foundation. *See* Kellogg
Foundation